FAEROE ISLANDS

SHETLAND ISLANDS

SWEDEN

NORWAY

FINLAND

LAKE LADOGA

AMULET FROM GNEZDOVO HOARD

OSEBERG SHIP

Oslo

Birka

Staraja Ladoga

CHESS PIECE

Oseberg

RUNE-STONE

Novgorod

DENMARK

LINDISFARNE ISLAND

Roskilde

BALTIC SEA

Gnezdovo

Hedeby

Dnieper River

York

ENGLAND

Dorestad

Rhine River

Dublin

London

Kiev

Don River

Paris

Volga River

Loire River

PITCHER AND BEAKER

Danube River

BLACK SEA

CASPIAN SEA

Rome

Constantinople

SILVER COINS

Seville

MEDITERRANEAN SEA

VIKINGS

RAIDERS FROM THE NORTH

TIME®
LIFE

LOST CIVILIZATIONS

This edition published in 2004
by the Caxton Publishing Group
20 Bloomsbury Street, London WC1B 3JH
Under license from Time-Life Books BV.

SERIES EDITOR: Dale M. Brown
Administrative Editor: Philip Brandt George

Editorial staff for *Vikings: Raiders From the North*
Art Director: Susan K. White
Cover Design: Open Door Limited, Rutland UK
Picture Editor: Kristin Baker Hanneman
Text Editors: James Michael Linch (principal), Charles J. Hagner
Writers: Denise Dersin
Associate Editor/Research: Jacqueline L. Shaffer
Assistant Editor/Research: Katherine L. Griffin
Assistant Art Director: Bill McKenney
Senior Copyeditor: Jarelle S. Stein
Picture Coordinator: David A. Herod
Editorial Assistant: Patricia D. Whiteford

Special Contributors: Ellen Galford, Donald Dale Jackson,
Harvey Loomis, Barbara Mallen, Valerie Moolman, Deborah Papier,
Daniel Stashower, David S. Thomson (text); Camille Fallow,
Maureen D. Lenihan, Gail Prensky, Eugenia S. Scharf, Lauren V. Scharf,
Ylann Schemm (research); Roy Nanovic (index)

Correspondents: Elisabeth Kraemer-Singh (Bonn), Christine Hinze
(London), Christina Lieberman (New York), Maria Vincenza Aloisi
(Paris), Ann Natanson (Rome). Valuable assistance was also provided
by Corky Bastlund, Ellen Vestergaard (Copenhagen); Judy Aspinall
(London); Juan Sosa (Moscow); Elizabeth Brown, Katheryn White
(New York); Dag Christensen (Oslo); Ann Wise (Rome); Mary Johnson
(Stockholm).

Title: *Vikings: Raiders From the North*
ISBN: 1 84447 054 7

The Consultants:

Professor Noel D. Broadbent, director of the Arctic Social Sciences
Program for the National Science Foundation in Washington, D.C.,
received his doctorate in Nordic archaeology from Sweden's
University of Uppsala.

Dr. Thomas H. McGovern specialises in the archaeology of the
Viking age settlers of Iceland and Greenland. He has directed Hunter
College's Bioarchaeology Facility since 1979.

Christopher D. Morris, professor of archaeology at the University
of Glasgow, has undertaken excavation and fieldwork on Viking sites
in the British Isles since 1974.

Dr. Marjorie Susan Venit is associate professor of art history
and archaeology at the University of Maryland and has published
extensively on the subject of ancient art.

Birgitta Linderoth Wallace directed the last year of the L'Anse
aux Meadows excavations as staff archaeologist for the Canadian
Parks Service and is preparing the report on the site.

This volume is one in a series that explores the worlds of the past,
using the finds of archaeologists and other scientists to bring ancient
peoples and their cultures vividly to life.

Other volumes included in the series:

LOST CIVILIZATIONS

VIKINGS

RAIDERS FROM THE NORTH

BY THE EDITORS OF TIME-LIFE BOOKS

CONTENTS

Under a glowering sky, sunlight reflects off the Nord Fjord, one of the major fjords cutting deep into Norway's rocky western coast. From sheltered spots like this, Viking raiders and merchants sailed forth into the world—"the blue water, smitten by many oars, foaming far and wide," as one 11th-century author put it—and altered the course of European history.

A PEOPLE BIGGER THAN LIFE

For generations, the Norwegian farm family had tilled their fertile plot near Gokstad along the shores of the Oslo Fjord without apparently giving much thought to the huge mound—fully 50 yards in diameter—situated on their property. With arable land at a premium in this mountainous country, they had plowed and cultivated the hillock until, by the late 19th century, it had dwindled to a height of 15 feet.

Although no record of its original dimensions exists, the large barrow of earth on the Gokstad farm had always been known as the King's Mound because a folk tale claimed that a king and all his treasure lay buried beneath it. The Oslo Fjord, in fact, was commonly referred to as the Valley of the Kings after the Swedish monarchs who had established small domains there a dozen centuries before. Perhaps the greatest surprise is that, in all that time, none of the locals had torn up the Gokstad mound in search of booty.

That all changed one day in April 1880, when the sons of the farmer decided to open up the mound. Whether they had seen something or struck an object with a plow is not known, but in any case they began to sink a shaft downward from the center of the mound, a haphazard and potentially destructive digging technique. News of their private enterprise soon reached Nikolas Nikolaysen, an eminent excavator and president of the Oslo Antiquarian Society, who sped

A curved serpent's head and elegant carving embellish the lofty prow of a Viking ship built circa AD 800 and excavated in 1904 from a burial mound near Oseberg in Norway.

to the scene on a rescue mission. He first halted the vertical digging, then he and his team drove a trench in from the side of the mound to avoid damaging whatever might lie within.

Remarkably, on their second day at the site, the excavators cleared away a thick layer of blue clay to reveal the prow of a mighty oaken ship in a superb state of preservation. Although Nikolaysen was delighted by the discovery, he was not entirely surprised: He had half-expected a ship burial—a Scandinavian practice dating back to the Bronze Age or even earlier—like hundreds of others found beneath Norwegian and Swedish mounds, many of which he had investigated himself. But this ship was unusually large and finely wrought, and as Nikolaysen scooped away the enveloping clay, he was convinced that it belonged to the Viking period.

Archaeological excavation in Norway is often held hostage by the country's northern location and coastal climate—short, dark winter days and frequent rain during much of the rest of the year. Yet, miraculously, for two months the sun shone on the Gokstad dig as Nikolaysen enlarged the original trench, his diggers working long into the evening hours under the oblique northern rays. The absence of rain, however, created its own problems as more and more of the ship was exposed. The impermeable clay had kept the timbers as sound and seaworthy as on the day of burial, but now they began to dry out and warp. To save the wood and reduce evaporation, Nikolaysen and his team drenched the ship in water at least once a day and covered the exposed parts with fresh-cut spruce boughs.

When the ship emerged, somewhat flattened and distorted by the weight of the earth and clay, it proved to be an elegantly crafted vessel measuring 76 feet from stem to stern. Based on its contents, Nikolaysen determined that it had been built around AD 850. Sixteen oar ports had been cut into each side, and covering them on the outside were the remnants of 32 three-foot battle shields.

It also became apparent that, despite the mound's unblemished outward appearance, someone had in fact searched it earlier for treasure: Ancient graverobbers had smashed through one side of the vessel and into what had been a square tent structure near the stern. Nikolaysen, following the thieves into the housing after hundreds of years, observed that he was in a burial chamber stripped of its riches but not of its occupant. The man had been about 50 years old, over six feet tall, and afflicted with gout—a conclusion based on the telltale deformation of the skeleton. Though his personal effects and weap-

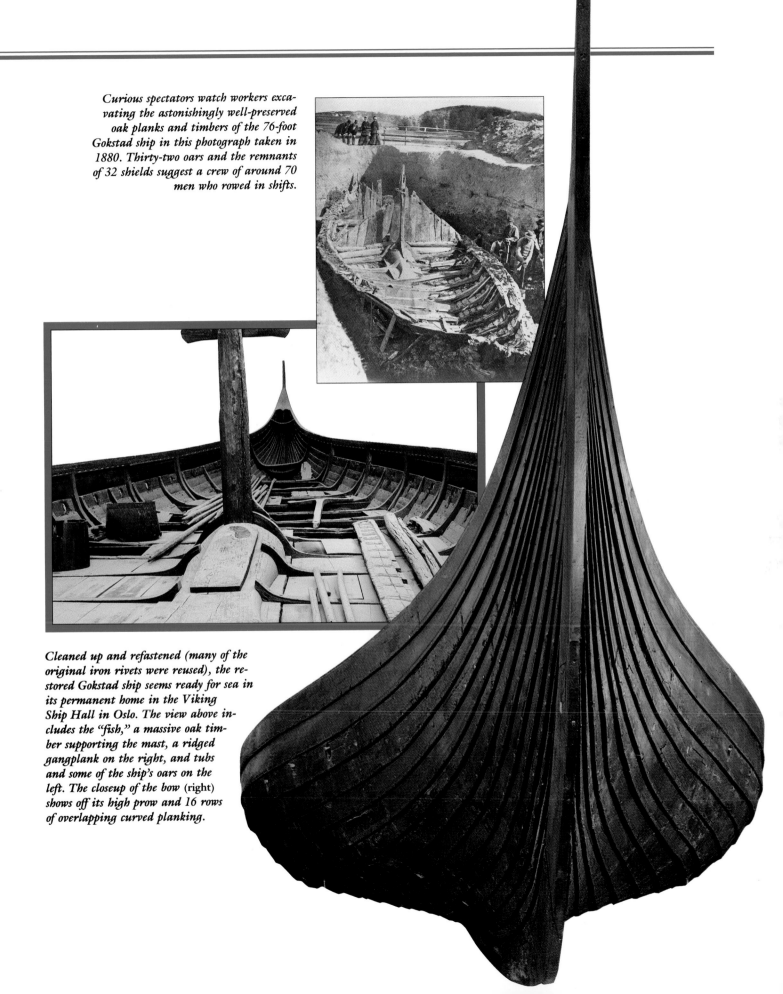

Curious spectators watch workers excavating the astonishingly well-preserved oak planks and timbers of the 76-foot Gokstad ship in this photograph taken in 1880. Thirty-two oars and the remnants of 32 shields suggest a crew of around 70 men who rowed in shifts.

Cleaned up and refastened (many of the original iron rivets were reused), the restored Gokstad ship seems ready for sea in its permanent home in the Viking Ship Hall in Oslo. The view above includes the "fish," a massive oak timber supporting the mast, a ridged gangplank on the right, and tubs and some of the ship's oars on the left. The closeup of the bow (right) shows off its high prow and 16 rows of overlapping curved planking.

SCANDINAVIA BEFORE THE VIKINGS: AN AGE OF TURMOIL AND GOLD

In the year AD 5, a Roman fleet sent by Caesar Augustus made landfall on the Jutland Peninsula, marking the first contact between Europe's foremost power and the Scandinavian tribes who were the Vikings' direct ancestors. Based on eyewitness reports from this and later voyages, Roman scholar Tacitus wrote the first credible account of a Norse people, the Svear, observing, among other things, that "the style of their ships is unusual in that there is a prow at each end." By the first century's close, he noted, the Svear of Uppland in Sweden—known for martial skills, devotion to wealth, and unswerving fealty—dominated the region.

A north-south pattern of commerce grew out of these early contacts, as demonstrated by Norse grave goods unearthed from this period. Up the trade routes and into Svear hands flowed the wealth of Rome and Byzantium, including ornamental brooches, vessels of silver and glass, and an abundance of gold Roman coins, called solidi.

When the Roman Empire collapsed in the fifth century, shock waves convulsed the Western world. Germanic tribes surged back and forth across Europe in search of spoils and better land, creating a fury of movement that led historians to describe the years 400 to 600 as the Migration Era. In Scandinavia, this time of turbulence was also an age of great wealth. Foreign trade continued, but goods were increasingly paid for with solidi, many of which Attila the Hun had extorted from the emperor Theodosius II before Rome's fall. Hoards of the one-ounce coins have turned up on the Baltic islands of Gotland, Öland, and Bornholm—Svear trading centers in the Migration Era—which also contain massive stone forts, suggesting that the age of gold was perilous as well as prosperous.

Most of the coins that flowed north into Sweden were melted down and fashioned into medallions, neck rings, and ornaments of exquisite artistry. But with the Roman gold mines no longer operative, the supply of solidi eventually exhausted itself, and Arab silver became increasingly the metal of choice.

The Romans used gold solidi—such as these from a hoard found on Bornholm near fire-blackened ruins of fifth-century farmhouses, perhaps destroyed by raiders—to pay Roman mercenaries, hence the derivation of the word soldier.

Roman emperors often struck heavy gold medallions, stamped on both sides, to present to allies and friends, Norse goldsmiths made facsimiles, called bracteates (left), frequently embossed on one side only.

This magnificent three-ringed collar, discovered at the foot of the Ålleberg Mountain in western Sweden, was created by a fifth-century Norse jeweler from melted-down Roman gold. With its perfection of detail and dramatic use of miniature human masks flanked by crouching animals, the piece embodies the finest Scandinavian craftsmanship of the Migration Era.

ons were missing, enough remained in and around the burial chamber to suggest what manner of man he was: a Viking warrior, a chieftain at least, perhaps indeed a king.

Several creatures had accompanied the man in death. The skeletons of 12 horses and the remnants of ornamental harnesses lay near the remains of six dogs and—surprisingly—the bones and feathers of a peacock, a rare import to these northern climes. As the work continued, the diggers found six beds, one with elaborately carved posts and others, easily dismantled, that might have served as camp beds. Scraps of woolen and silk textiles interwoven with gold thread remained as an indication of long-lost finery. Whatever jewelry there might have been was gone, but much of value to archaeologists remained—oars, an anchor, three small dinghylike boats, several iron-bound sea chests, and the framework of the tent with its pole tops carved into dragon heads. And there was more—kegs and barrels, with contents vanished, wooden mugs and plates, a great iron cauldron large enough to hold food for 50, even a games cabinet including a checkerboard to while away the hours of a voyage to eternity.

The Gokstad vessel had once been a fine seagoing ship. Hewn from a tall, straight oak tree, the keel had been curved to bear the greatest weight amidships and its ends tapered to streamline passage. Ribs were of solid oak, cut from naturally curved pieces painstakingly shaped to suit their keel position. These were covered by strakes, or planking, made from one-inch-thick sections of overlapping oak, nailed to the ribs and lashed together with spruce-root cordage. The result was a fast-moving, flexible craft, ideal for sudden hit-and-run raids on distant targets. More than just a fast warship, it was a work of art, a superb example of the skill of a Viking shipwright.

Using historical sources, scholars even believe they have identified the body in the Gokstad ship. In the 1920s Professor Anton Willem Brøgger of the University of Oslo asserted that the man was King Olaf Gudrodson, gout-ridden son of the elderly king Gudrod of Vestvold. Here, wonderfully well preserved, was not only a key to the Viking raids but a window into the world of a seagoing chieftain, the theme of his existence borne out in death, when the ship of his life's adventures carried him to the afterworld.

Well before the end of the eighth century the ship had become the ubiquitous symbol of the Viking spirit. Flotillas of vessels that were manned by formidable warriors yelling battle cries descended on

EVOLUTION OF THE LONGSHIP

The ships that carried Vikings to Europe, North Africa, Asia Minor, and North America were aesthetic and technological marvels, built by expert shipwrights whose doorstep was the sea itself. An extraordinary series of archaeological finds has provided a vivid record of the evolution of the Viking ship from the 4th century BC up through the 11th century AD. Some of the developments appear in the boats illustrated at right, which are arranged in chronological order and shown in cross section as well as in side view, with length indicated by the scale at the bottom.

Viking ships can be broken down into two distinct categories: those that were designed for raids and travel, and those designed for transportation of cargo. The war and travel vessels tended to be light and narrow for speed, with oar ports along their sides. Easily lowered sails allowed rowers to take over when greater maneuverability was needed. By contrast, cargo boats were high and wide and the mast fixed. But both types shared a basic construction technique. Planks, or strakes, were overlaid, fixed to the frame with iron rivets, and caulked with cordage made from animal hair and plant material.

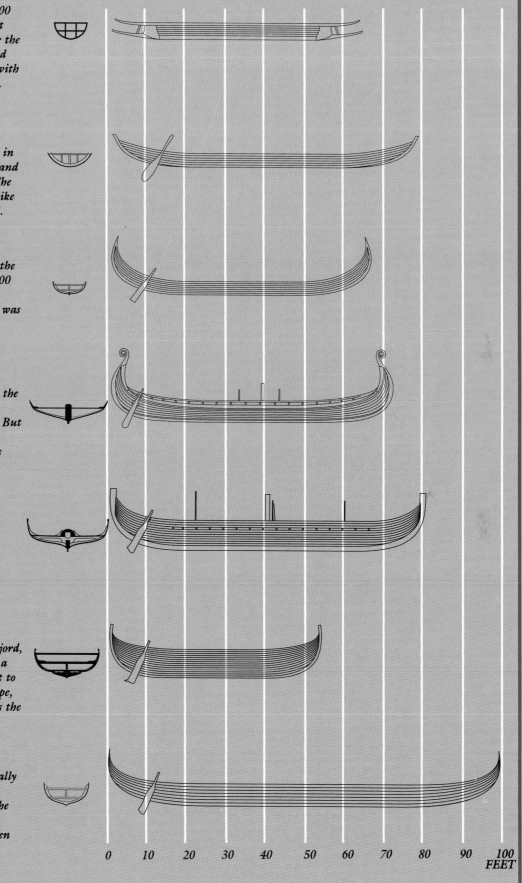

Dating from between 500 and 300 BC, the Danish Hjortspring boat was built with a broad plank for the bottom and two on each side, held together with cord and caulked with resin. It was paddled, not rowed.

The planks of the Nydam vessel, which was built around AD 350 in Denmark, ran the hull's length and were fastened with iron rivets. The vessel was propelled by oars but like the Hjortspring boat had no sail.

From a bog in western Norway, the Kvalsund vessel of around AD 700 had a true keel, which made it stronger than its predecessors. It was also broader, for its length, and probably had a mast and sail.

Built between AD 800 and 850, the famous Oseberg ship is the most beautiful Viking ship yet found. But its delicate construction and low sides suggest that its mission was more ceremonial than warlike.

The strong Gokstad ship, circa AD 850, had a solid keel, wide beam, and a 42-foot mast for its square sail. A steering oar was mounted aft on the right side.

Found in Denmark's Roskilde Fjord, Skuldelev Wreck 1 was a knorr, a high-sided merchant vessel, built to haul cargo and livestock. The type, which favored sail over oars, was the workhorse of the Viking fleet.

Skuldelev Wreck 2 is only partially reconstructed, but is the longest Viking ship found so far. Like the Wreck 1, it dates from about AD 1000, and it would have been used on overseas raids.

0   10   20   30   40   50   60   70   80   90   100
FEET

foreign coasts from Ireland to Byzantium and all points in between, killing and plundering.

Terrified Europeans wondered what manner of ships these were that brought such violence to their shores. The vessels could appear unexpectedly on the horizon and approach so swiftly that residents barely had time to flee. With their shallow draft and flexible framework, Viking boats often drew right up onto the beach to disgorge their howling crews. And who were the men that manned the vessels, that they could navigate across open sea with such remarkable stealth and skill?

These ferocious raiders were Norsemen, or Scandinavians—a collective name for the peoples of Norway, Denmark, Sweden, and part of Finland. Water was, for most of them, their natural element. From earliest times the inhabitants of the heavily forested, mountainous lands of the North had worked the soil wherever it was productive and plied their coasts, rivers, fjords, and lakes in search of fish and trade.

In the early eighth century, inspired shipwrights learned to add masts, sails, and stable keels to coastal craft, and local watermen saw an opportunity to venture to far more distant lands. Their ships gave them

Archaeologist Gabriel Gustafson, third from left, stands with his crew in a 1904 photograph of the Oseberg ship excavation. Among the many items buried with the ship were 30 oars. The damaged stern and prow sections would be reconstructed from fragments.

direct access to the markets of Europe and, through intermediaries, to the world beyond. The Norsemen became adept at foreign trade with the British Isles, Russia, Italy, and France. Later they turned to brigandage against many of their erstwhile business partners.

Both raiding and trading motivated the more adventuresome, for the definition of wealth changed—as contacts with the outside world grew—from agricultural output to possession of precious metals, predominantly silver. This type of wealth provided the key to acquisition of land, and land was the source of power and prestige. Since family holdings generally passed to the firstborn son, subsequent male offspring who hoped to own property at home had to

Among the several sleds recovered from the Oseberg ship was the one at upper right, shown as found, and the reconstructed one at right, which measures about seven feet long.

16

make their fortunes first, generally on foreign soil. Many of these Norsemen ultimately settled overseas, establishing Viking colonies in Russia, France, Scotland, Iceland, Greenland, and Canada.

These adventurers depended utterly on their ships to carry them safely to far-off realms. Not surprisingly, the ship as an emblem of Vikinghood is everywhere in Norse lore and has also bequeathed to the modern world some of the best-preserved relics of the Viking age. Adding directly to the social history that can be gleaned from the ships themselves and the artifacts they held are inscriptions and chronicles of various sorts. Enraged European clerics of Viking times wrote about the piracy and butchery of the pagan Norsemen. Arab merchants rubbing shoulders with Viking traders in the marketplaces of the world wrote their own colorful—and sometimes scornful— accounts. The saga writers of Iceland, collecting folk memories and fragments of poetry some 200 to 300 years after the events, preserved the spirit of their ancestors but embellished deeds and reputations for dramatic effect and in order to please descendants. Only the rune-stones—carved inscriptions in an alphabet of 16 characters suitable merely for abbreviated but important messages—speak in the Vikings' own words *(pages 28-29)*.

What *was* a Viking? The derivation of the term is unknown. It generally—and generically—includes all Scandinavians of the period from the mid-eighth century, when they began to venture beyond home ports, to the year 1066, when the Battle of Hastings led to the conquest of England, a watershed in European history. Yet technically, the term applies only to raiders. To go "a-Viking" meant

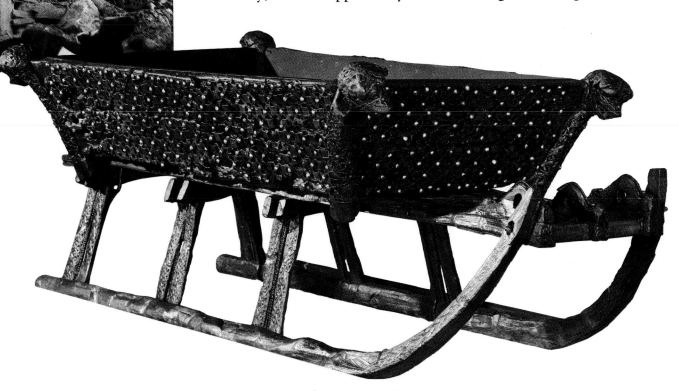

to go forth on expeditions down the fjords and across the seas to acquire riches and a reputation at home for being a doer of deeds— the two things most important in the life of the Scandinavian male.

Not quite 25 years after the excavation at Gokstad, another farmer, some 10 miles away at Oseberg, Norway, began to explore a large mound on his land. Finding some sort of wood construction, he continued digging until he identified part of an ancient ship. He had unearthed what remained of the mast and was down to the roof of an apparent cabin before having second thoughts and calling upon expert help. Professor Gabriel Gustafson, director of the Oslo University Collection of Antiquities, began a preliminary excavation that soon convinced him he was onto an important ship burial.

In the following year, 1904, Gustafson went to work with a full team of skilled assistants. Almost at once he found the sternpost of a large ship, a single piece of fine oak intricately carved—far more exquisite than anything on the Gokstad ship. The burial chamber of this vessel, too, had been plundered. Discarded fragments of the robbers' spoils lay scattered alongside the hull. Also found, tossed out without ceremony, were the skeletons of the chamber's occupants: two women, one about 50, the other perhaps 30 years of age. They had been handled, as an assistant of Gustafson's noted tersely, "with shocking regardlessness." But not ignored, for the skeleton of the older woman was missing a right hand and wrist, the fingers of the left hand, and the upper left arm. The archaeologists deduced that the thieves had lopped the parts off for their precious rings and bracelets.

The implications were fascinating. Here was a ship almost as large as the Gokstad find, though lighter and less solidly constructed—as if it had been built some time before shipwrights had discovered the secret of the most efficient hull shape—but far more lavishly appointed. Altogether, it appeared less seaworthy and more ornamental than would be required of a fighting ship. Scholars speculated that it could have been a ceremonial vessel or, perhaps, a royal yacht for cruising local waters. To date the Oseberg burial has provided the richest haul of Viking-age grave goods. And the occupants were women. One of the two must have been an individual of great wealth and power to merit such a burial; the other probably was a servant. The elaborate burial proved that a woman could achieve great wealth and high status in Norway and suggested that this particular woman

A WELL-PROVISIONED JOURNEY TO DEATH FOR THE NORSE OF VENDEL AND VALSGÄRDE

Peace and a more settled kind of prosperity came to Scandinavia at the end of the Migration Era. In Sweden's Uppland, luxury-loving Svear chieftains bedecked themselves with resplendent helmets, inlaid swords, and superbly fashioned gilded ornaments from abroad.

In the 1880s archaeologists discovered abundant evidence of this opulent lifestyle when they excavated 14 remarkable graves in the Vendel district north of the city of Stockholm. Each of the graves marked the last resting place of a chieftain who was buried in his ship with all his finery around him. In the 1920s, 15 additional ship burials were found at nearby Valsgärde—a virtual armada at anchor in the soil. Most of the more splendid graves at both sites date to the seventh and eighth centuries, a time now referred to as the Vendel era.

The greatest treasures among the Vendel grave goods are headgear made of iron and bronze, shields, swords, chain-mail shirts, and lavish horse gear. Most compelling of these are the helmets, which share general features at the crown and forehead but differ over the face.

Contrary to popular belief, neither the Vendel-era warriors nor those who came after them wore horned helmets. In fact, these ubiquitous symbols of Vikinghood belong to the Bronze Age—1500 to 500 BC —when they served as ceremonial headgear for priests at fertility rites.

Unearthed in a Valsgärde grave, this richly wrought iron helmet of a Vendel-era chieftain no doubt struck terror into the hearts of his foes. The crest, visor, and stamped panels crossing the cap are of bronze, the beardlike face shield of iron.

Excavated in the summer of 1933, the remaining traces in a Valsgärde ship grave known as Number 7 *(below)* suggest that this vessel—which might have been equipped with a sail—was lightweight, easily handled, and suitable for plying inland rivers or hoisting into the Baltic for sea trips. Its contents, including the decorative weaponry of an esteemed warrior, rank among the richest and most evocative of all known boat burials in the pre-Viking age.

Fully one-third of the craft contained food stores and kitchen equipment. In the bow were fire tongs, a roasting spit, a frying pan, and a great iron cauldron large enough to feed an entire crew. Meat joints of domestic animals and the bones of wild game birds filled the galley. Outside the ship lay the skeletal remains of yet more supplies: unbutchered carcasses of beasts apparently slaughtered on the spot. Near a full-grown young ox and a large boar lay four horses, their bones still draped in richly decorated bridles. The stern *(far right)*, which curiously was empty, may have held perishable items, such as wineskins.

As had happened in previous excavations of Vendel-era burials at Valsgärde, not a single human skeleton was found. However, substantial remnants of pillows and other bedding were discovered amidships, suggesting that a body had been present.

Traces of bone—reduced to nothing more than powder—were located and subsequently tested. Laboratory analysis confirmed that the animal skeletons had remained relatively intact because the beasts had been freshly killed at the site and because their bones were young and calcium rich. But the human occupant had been older, with a lower calcium content in his bones. Moreover, he had probably lain in state prior to interment, perhaps over a period of weeks or even months. His death in winter, when the earth was frozen hard, would have postponed burial. Whatever the case, his body, after prolonged exposure to air, would have decomposed faster than had it been sealed in the ground.

The drawing at right by a member of the archaeological team at Valsgärde depicts the extensive array of artifacts—including numerous iron rivets—uncovered at ship burial Number 7. The pattern formed by the rivets permitted the artist to reconstruct the shape of the vessel.

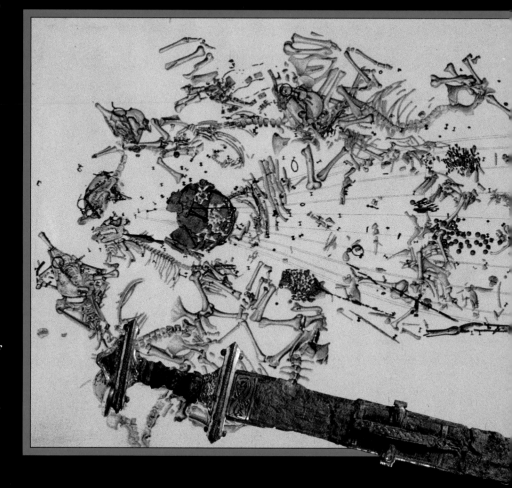

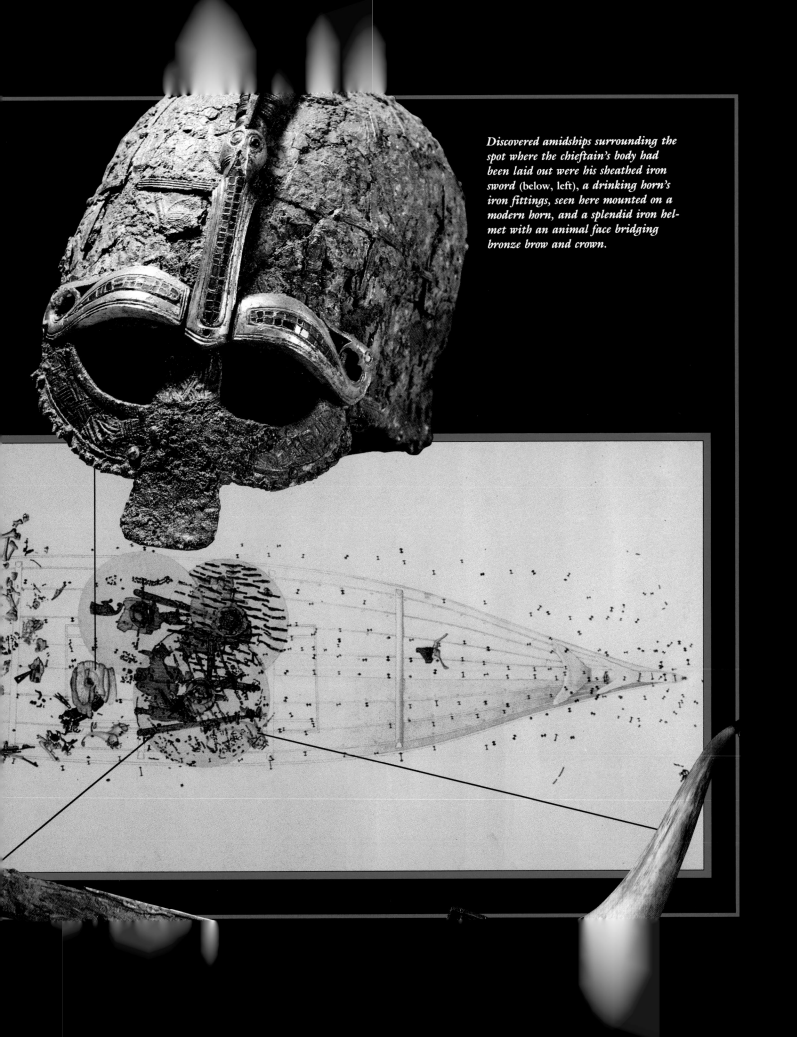

Discovered amidships surrounding the spot where the chieftain's body had been laid out were his sheathed iron sword (below, left), a drinking horn's iron fittings, seen here mounted on a modern horn, and a splendid iron helmet with an animal face bridging bronze brow and crown.

might have been a queen. Yet however important she may have been in life, she had known that she could not be with her menfolk in death; Valhalla, the afterworld, was strictly segregated by sex.

As at Gokstad, a stratum of blue clay had encapsulated and preserved the Oseberg ship, although the weight of the mound had crushed much of the woodwork of the more delicate vessel. When the archaeologists finally sorted out the thousands of burial items and ship fragments, there was no longer any doubt that the occupants must have come from a royal house. But the question of the women's identities remained. A. W. Brøgger, who had previously identified the Gokstad remains, believed the sagas and the mound contents, taken together, provided the answer. According to Brøgger, one of the Oseberg women was almost certainly Queen Asa, stepmother of Gokstad's gout-ridden King Olaf Gudrodson and grandmother of the future king Harald Fairhair, unifier of all Norway.

For their journey to the other world the Oseberg women had been supplied with several beds, complete with eiderdown quilts and cushions. A chair, two lamps, some tapestries, and spinning and weaving implements provided comfort and occupation for the voyagers. In case land travel and camping proved necessary, there were four finely carved sleds, an ornate four-wheeled carriage, two large tents, and a dozen horses, represented by their skeletal remains. Among the more personal belongings were combs, a pair of scissors, a thread box, and two pairs of fine calfskin shoes apparently specially made for a woman with arthritic feet. In and around the galley of the death ship were such everyday utensils as an iron cauldron, a kettle, frying pans, and kitchen knives. Food for the voyage

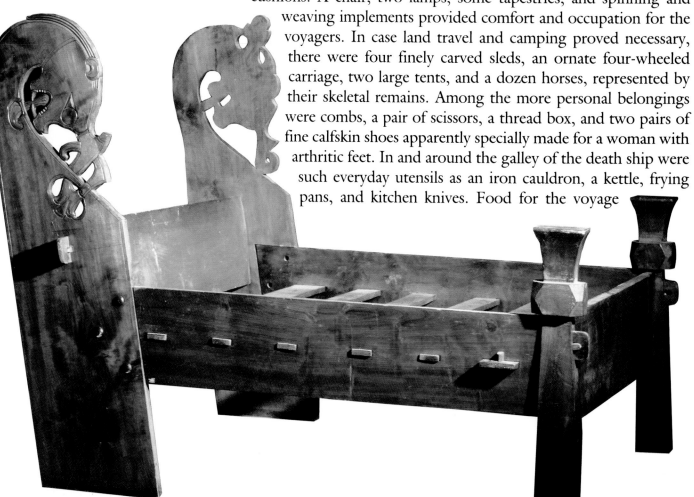

A 5½-foot bed with stylized animal-head posts was one of the many objects included in the Oseberg burial mound to ensure the royal occupant's comfort in the other world. The original was too decayed to be rebuilt, but this copy shows how the bed could be taken apart for stowage aboard ship during voyages.

included meat—a young bull, now only bones—dough for bread, and, in one chest, wheat and some wild apples. To season this fare, the ship's stores included cumin, mustard, and horseradish.

While the relics recovered from the Oseberg and Gokstad burials illuminate the ways of the wealthy and powerful, they shed little light on the everyday lives of ordinary folk in the Viking age. Because the Vikings built their homesteads mainly of wood, there is little left but postholes and trenches in patterns evoking the outlines of disintegrated structures. Yet, working patiently with the evidence at hand, in recent years archaeologists have assembled a picture of farmers and villagers that makes those who stayed at home seem a whole lot less barbaric than do the accounts of the Vikings' enemies and detractors.

Since the 1970s numerous excavations have yielded ground plans of farms and villages and revealed a mass of information about daily life. Supporting verification comes from surviving farm tools and fishing equipment and from as seemingly ephemeral clues as carbonized grain and animal bones. No opportunity has gone ignored: The scientists even excavated a field in Denmark, covered by windblown sand in Viking times, that still bore the footprints of farmers and animals, the tracks of carts, and the furrows made by a plow. Underwater archaeology has extended knowledge of the Vikings still further *(pages 39-49)*. At Hedeby, in Denmark, for example, tar brushes made of scraps of cloth were retrieved from the harbor where they had been tossed by Viking shipwrights. When examined, they revealed much about Viking clothing.

Such information has helped corroborate many details of life spelled out in the 10th-century poem *Rigsthula*. Most people of the

Buried with the Oseberg ship was this royal 18-foot wagon, the only wheeled vehicle to survive intact from Viking times. There were few roads in ninth-century Norway but many waterways, and the cart's richly carved body was designed to be lifted from the chassis and put directly aboard a boat.

Another household item found in the Oseberg ship burial was this elaborate chest, made of oak and reinforced by iron bands studded with nailheads. It is four feet long and 16 inches high—its legs were pegged into the bottom plank—and was probably used to store domestic items.

Viking age survived not by launching raids on the rest of Europe but by raising livestock and tilling the soil. They hunted, fished, and opportunistically gathered wild plants, honey, and eggs. But their own land and nearby waters supplied almost all their needs, from fish and meat to clothing. According to *Rigsthula,* the farmer's life was indeed a busy one. Farmers "tamed the oxen, tempered plough-shares, timbered houses and barns for the hay, fashioned carts, and followed the plough." They also chopped down forests and cleared them of stones, often leaving the latter in scattered little piles that puzzled archaeologists many centuries later. What could these cairns be? They were much too small for grave mounds. Studies of the surface and below-surface soil showed unmistakable evidence of cultivation and of the stones having been heaped up here and there as they were dislodged by farmers working their fields. The inference seems clear; farmers, especially in rocky Norway, needed all of the land that their plows could turn.

Climatologists have determined that Scandinavia was several degrees warmer during the Viking period than in earlier or later times. Upland areas, used only for summer grazing before, could be farmed year-round. More successful agriculture spurred an expansion of population, both in numbers and in territory. Prior to the foreign-trade boom, the society measured wealth in terms of animal and grain production, creating competition between landowners for more land and a surge of violence by have-nots attempting to become haves. Meanwhile, in the eye of the storm, the simple farmer—the backbone of the Viking world—quietly pursued life's daily tasks.

These were for the most part not isolated farmsteads. Recent archaeological excavations, primarily in the central Jutland area of Denmark, show that clusters of farmsteads rather than single farms predominated throughout Scandinavia. Such villages were made up of six to eight farms, each one with its own living quarters, barns, workshops, and storerooms.

The workday of a typical farm family began before daylight, when the father and his older sons went into the fields to plow or plant cereal crops, while the women and the younger children tended

Based on a Swedish excavation of a 10th-century farm, this drawing of a long house suggests how closely the Viking farmer's life was tied to the land. At left is the feed storage and cattle barn, then the kitchen and living quarters, with two raised hearths. At right is the grain barn, where cereal crops were threshed, cleaned, and stored.

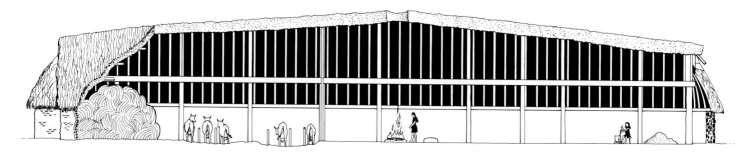

The excavation of a 250-foot long house, home of an early Viking chieftain, appears as a light-brown rectangle in the lower-left of this aerial view of the Norwegian island Vestvågøy. Though living north of the Arctic Circle, he owned gold and silver items and jugs and glass from Europe, as evidenced by the dig.

The floor plan of the same Viking house as at left shows postholes for the supports that held up the structure's thatched roof. The double posts divided the house into its three parts. At center are the two hearths. Eating and sleeping platforms probably lined the living area's walls, which were made of wattle and daub covered with birch bark.

the cattle, goats, pigs, and geese. The primary focus was on animal husbandry. Hay—to keep the livestock alive through the winter—was grown, cut, and stored no matter what else was harvested. One archaeologist has calculated that in Norway, with the least available farmland of the Scandinavian countries, the entire grain crop went into the brewing of beer, a nourishing as well as social beverage that was almost as important as milk.

As excavations have revealed, a farming unit usually consisted of a cluster of houses and outbuildings loosely encircled by a fence or crude stone wall. In most cases the main dwelling was a long, rectangular structure of wood, sod, or wattle and daub, interwoven branches and twigs covered by clay; at one end were the living quarters and at the other cattle stalls, the animals offering a welcome source of heat during winter. An open hearth, probably slightly raised above the earthen floor in the center of the living quarters, supplied warmth and some light, which could be supplemented by seal-oil lamps. Elevated platforms along the side walls provided both seating and sleeping accommodations near the fire. The house had no chimney, only a hole in the roof to let the smoke out.

In this one long room, the farm family cooked, ate, entertained their friends, churned their butter, worked their looms, fashioned shafts for their arrows, made love, and slept. Presiding over its dim and no doubt smoky interior was the family patriarch, proprietor of the farm, who was ever ready to demonstrate his wealth and generosity to friends and neighbors by serving feasts of spitted meats, fish, breads, vegetables, and huge quantities of beer, mead, and fermented fruit wines.

Moving purposefully through the scene was the family matriarch, undisputed mistress of the household. But the furnishing and maintenance of the main house's great, all-purpose living space composed only a small part of her responsibilities. On any day she might be seen at work on the family property wearing at her waist her own badge of office, the bunch of keys that secured the main house, sheds, barns, the separate storehouses for preserved and perishable foods, and the bathhouse or steamhouse if the farmstead was rich enough

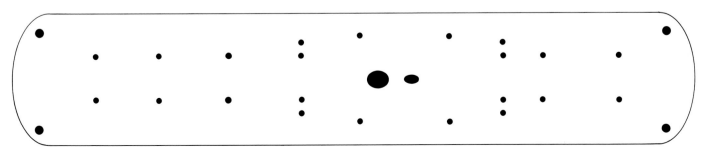

to possess such a luxury. She also spun thread, wove, milked the cows, churned the butter, and made the cheese.

Around the home the wife supervised her daughters in their household duties, which included baking, food preparation, and mending clothes and bedding. Not until almost midmorning did the men come in to be served the first meal of the day on the narrow tables in the central hall; porridge with buttermilk, eaten out of wooden bowls, and a serving of dried mutton or perhaps fresh fish. Afterward, the family rested for a brief period and then returned to their duties; at the end of the workday the second and final meal was served. This would be no more sumptuous than the first, except that there would be great quantities of beer.

In some ways, women enjoyed a status unknown in most parts of the world at that time. Arab visitors to Viking communities in the 10th century noted with astonishment that wives were remarkably free in the marital state. "The right to divorce belongs to the women," wrote one man disapprovingly. "The wife divorces whenever she wishes." Not only that: The dowry was refundable if the marriage ended in divorce. By law, women could own land and very often were left to manage it alone while their husbands went off to barter for needed goods or ventured overseas on trading or raiding expeditions. Indeed, rune-stones testify to the women's utilitarian skills if not to the undying love of their mates. The husband of a woman named Odindisa of Västmanland in Sweden offered this no-nonsense burial tribute: "There will not come to Hassmyra a better mistress who holds sway over the farm." A good manager was Odindisa and, as such, would be sorely missed.

Land was status and prosperity; land was a power base. All men aspired to become landholders; but few of them could, and those few usually not without an apprenticeship in trading or raiding. Contrary to popular belief, the aggressive pillagers of the eighth century were not the ones who launched the Viking age. Modern archaeologists contend that the pirates who sacked foreign ports knew where they were going because they had been there before. "Probably," says Christian Keller, senior scholar in the department of archaeology at the University of Oslo, "they had been there about 50 to a hundred years earlier on more peaceful commerce, trading and bartering, bringing back objects and coins that

Art and function were skillfully fused in this whalebone plaque, decorated with carved animal heads, from a Viking grave in Norway. The 13½-inch-high plaque probably belonged to a wealthy woman, who may have used it to press pleats into wet linen cloth, folded and wound around it. The glass ball probably served to smooth out seams in cloth.

we have been able to date to long before the raids."

Overland trade, from eastern Europe and from Asia, had started even earlier. In about AD 600 or perhaps even 550, pre-Viking merchants had begun to establish a series of trade centers along the main lines of commerce through the Scandinavian countries: Birka in Sweden, Kaupang in southern Norway, the island of Gotland in the Baltic, and ultimately Hedeby in what was then Danish territory. These were, says archaeologist Thomas McGovern of New York City's Hunter College, "large emporia," occupied by no more than a core of people year-round but bustling with activity during the trading season—"sort of like giant trade fairs." The northern markets took place generally in late winter when a reduction in farm chores provided some free time and when ice skates (which the Vikings called "ice legs"), skis, and sleds facilitated easy travel and transport. Found by archaeologists in great numbers throughout Scandinavia, ice skates were generally made from horses' foot bones, which were smoothed on one side and fastened on with straps threaded through holes drilled in the bones.

Celts, Franks, Saxons, Slavs, and Arabs brought their various attitudes, standards, and ideologies to these emporia. They bartered such goods as silver, silks, wine, and swords and took home the furs, amber, leatherware, and ornaments of the local artisans. These polyglot traders made note—often in unflattering terms—of their hosts and their social customs. One visitor from Moorish Córdoba, a curmudgeon named Ibrahim al-Tartushi, characterized the extremely prosperous and cosmopolitan trade mart of Hedeby at about 950 as follows: "The town is poorly provided with property or treasure. The inhabitants' principal food is fish, which is plentiful. The people often throw a newborn child into the sea rather than maintain it."

Religious practices of the locals were particularly repulsive to al-Tartushi. "A feast is held to honor their deity and to eat and drink," he wrote. "Any man who slaughters a sacrificial animal—whether it is an ox, ram, goat, or pig—fastens it up on poles outside his house to show that he has made his sacrifice." As if all that were not unpleasant enough, the critic encountered something even more

The glass beads of this necklace, found in a 10th-century Norwegian grave, probably came from Italy. They were made by fusing glass rods of different colors into various combinations.

displeasing—the Norsemen at play. "I have never heard such horrible singing," he observed with disgust. "It is like a growl coming out of their throats, like the barking of dogs only still more brutish."

Al-Tartushi paints a one-sided portrait of Hedeby, but it is not unlikely that Viking-age merchants on long trading expeditions to markets well beyond Scandinavia and at trade fairs both at home and abroad would be roistering and raucous enough to offend fastidious entrepreneurs from more sophisticated societies, particularly Muslim Arabs from Spain. Yet different eyes saw different things. Even al-Tartushi found the Hedeby people beautiful and skillful in the use of cosmetics. "There is an artificial make-up for the eyes," he noted. "When they use it beauty never fades; on the contrary, it increases in men and women as well." English visitors, whose observations were transcribed from older sources by the 12th-century chronicler John of Wallingford some time after the Viking age, were quite impressed by the quality of Viking manhood. They spoke of men who bathed on Saturdays, combed their hair, dressed handsomely, and were therefore enviably successful with women.

Archaeological finds suggest that the men were indeed striking and well groomed—at least on their better days. From the evidence of their skeletal remains, they stood, on average, 5 feet 7¾ inches tall, with their leaders tending to reach 6 feet or more. The wagon salvaged from the Oseberg ship burial was decorated with three-dimensional renditions of male heads, meticulously carved to show details of carefully tended hair, neatly trimmed beards, and impressive, upward-curving mustaches culminating in tight little plaits. Excavated toilet articles confirm the impression that the Vikings cared about their looks. Diggers at grave sites have found

This rune-inscribed rock, from Hillersjö in Sweden, is one of the finest of the 5,000-odd examples of runic inscriptions that survive the Viking age. The runes, flowing in an intricate serpentine pattern, tell of a woman who inherited her daughter's estate. It confirms a feature of Viking society that was most liberal for the time—the prerogative of women to possess property in their own right.

Several runic alphabets known as futharks for their first six letters evolved among Germanic tribes, starting around the 1st century AD or slightly before. These 16 characters—shown with their phonetic sounds—constitute the Danish, or Common, futhark. Since runes were first inscribed in wood, they have no curved or horizontal strokes, as these would be harder to carve in the grain.

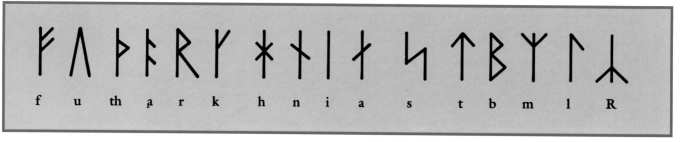

f u th ą r k h n i a s t b m l R

More than 800 runes are carved on five sides of this famed seven-foot-tall Swedish monument. They extol the nobility of a ninth-century king named Thiodrik. But runes were not just for kings. Archaeologists have found many small pieces of wood and bone casually carved with mundane runic messages, including "Kiss me."

quantities of combs (used not just for grooming but for removing lice), many of them beautifully decorated, as well as elegant washbowls and more prosaic things such as tweezers and ear scoops. Even teeth from the graves show signs of personal attention in the form of vigorous use of toothpicks.

But clean or not, handsome or not, Vikings on the rampage were a terrible force to be reckoned with. They frequently turned on each other in raids just as grisly as those they would later unleash against the rest of Europe. "I've been with sword and spear slippery with bright blood where kites wheeled," runs one 10th-century poem. "And how well we violent Vikings clashed! Red flames ate up men's roofs, raging we killed and killed, and skewered bodies sprawled sleepy in town gateways."

Even the northern religion was bellicose, resounding to the roll of thunder and the clash of mighty swords. The Viking pantheon embraced three major deities: Odin, father of the gods; Thor; and Frey. Odin, sometimes spelled Wotan or Wodan, wielded a spear and was the war god. Odin the wise, who had given up one eye in exchange for wisdom, was also god of creation and strife, god of poetry and the occult, god of the dead. Thor was the giant-killer, fighter for the forces of good, the guardian of justice. His symbol—the hammer—represented the lightning bolt. He was the sky god, god of thunder, ruler of winds, rains, and crops, noisy champion of humankind. The most mild-mannered of the trio was Frey, chief among many gods of fertility and plenty, whose likeness was depicted by his worshipers as a gigantic phallus. These three, as well as the other lesser gods, walked abroad among humans, influencing the

This exquisite silver amulet from 10th-century Sweden represents the hammer of Thor, son of the chief god Odin. Admired for his great strength, Thor combated evil, using his mighty hammer to do so.

Evil glowers from this seventh-century bronze brooch representing Thor's eternal enemy, the World Serpent. In Norse legend, the serpent lurked in the ocean, coiled around the earth. Thor finally killed the serpent in an epic fight but then fell dead, poisoned by its venom.

affairs of mortals and engaging in almost constant conflict with an array of giants and dwarfs and evil monsters.

Foreign visitors on occasion glimpsed Vikings at worship in the open air or in temples presided over by monumental images of the gods. Local farmers would gather for festivals, the foreigners noted, bringing huge quantities of food and drink and farm animals to be sacrificed. The blood of horses and cattle was captured in bowls and sprinkled not only over an entire temple but upon the worshipers as well. Meanwhile, the flesh was cooked up in cauldrons, for consumption by the assembled company to the accompaniment of many bibulous toasts to Odin and other favorite gods and to the memory of dead kin. From what the foreigners could gather, the afterlife was not well defined. It seemed that on the one hand the dead would exist in their grave mounds and that on the other they would journey to an other world. For the common folk that world might be a dull one, scarcely worth the trip. For noble warriors it was Valhalla, a male paradise of feasting and fighting enjoyed by gods, Valkyries, and heroes until the final cataclysmic loss to the forces of evil—and the end of the world.

All this was, of course, anathema to the Vikings' Christian and Muslim visitors. To them, the Viking religion was flamboyant but violent and depressing, offering no hope of ultimate redemption. Viking art reflected this grim ideology. It, too, was ferocious, full of power and frequently violence, yet possessed of a vigorous beauty all its own *(pages 77-85)*.

If foreign missionaries had failed to convert the northern pagans—and they had tried—the traveling merchants came much closer to succeeding. Many local traders discovered that they would have a far better chance of doing business with visiting Christian merchants if they allowed themselves to be blessed with the sign of the cross and earnestly announced their allegiance to Christ. In many cases they did not have to be baptized, so as to avoid offending their own gods; but if they did—so be it, they were baptized. Repeatedly, if need be. As often as the demands of trade required—and as often as white baptismal robes were being handed out free.

MODERN VIKING VOYAGES

The bold seagoing Viking spirit of a millennium ago has never really waned. In 1893 a latter-day Viking by the name of Magnus Andersen sailed a replica of the Gokstad ship from Bergen, Norway, to Newfoundland in 27 days.

Ninety-eight years later, a similar feat was carried off by 20th-century Scandinavians whose ship, the *Gaia (below)*, named for the earth mother, was also modeled on the Gokstad vessel. Some modern amenities, such as diesels, electronic navigational gear, and cabins for shelter, provided a margin of safety and comfort that the original Gokstad ship's mariners would have envied.

Yet the venture's basic mission—to build a ship just as the Vikings did *(right)* and sail her across the northern ocean as they did—was achieved with gala success. *Gaia* left the port of Bergen on May 17, 1991, and after stops in Iceland and Greenland arrived on August 2 at L'Anse aux Meadows, Newfoundland, where archaeological research shows Leif Eiriksson had landed around AD 1000. *Gaia* encountered strong winds and high waves—as Leif undoubtedly had—and, even with radar, it suffered some damage from floating ice. "Imagine what it would have been like," said the skipper of the *Gaia*, Norwegian Ragnar

Thorseth, "without radar on a dark and frozen sea."

As the Vikings well knew, the sea is indeed a hard master. Two other Viking replicas, *Oseberg* and *Saga Siglar,* joined *Gaia* in Canada in 1991 for a triumphal tour of North America's eastern coast. Then in the autumn of 1992 *Oseberg* and *Saga Siglar,* sailing off the coast of Spain, were overcome by high seas and sank, although their sailors were rescued. Many Viking ships suffered the same fate—but their crews would not have been so lucky.

Sporting signal flags, Gaia *sails into Canadian waters after her 1991 ocean crossing. The cabins are a modern concession to crew comfort.*

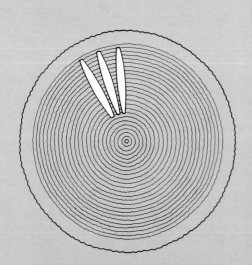

Instead of sawing wood into planks, Viking shipwrights split curving tree trunks lengthwise along the grain to get boards that were thin and pliable but preserved the natural strength of the wood.

Modern Norwegian shipbuilders work on Gaia's hull, building from the keel up. Overlapping planks go on first; frames, knees, and cross braces for strengthening the hull go in later. For authenticity, the builders used no modern tools—only those their forebears would have used: ax, chisel, adz, plane, drawknife, and auger.

Social structure in the land of the Vikings did not offer equal opportunity to all. Though class distinctions were not absolute, they clearly separated the masses from the most likely to succeed. Slaves, or thralls, occupied the lowest rung of the social ladder, although they did not necessarily start there. From bankrupts to prisoners of war to the sons and daughters of slaves, they performed the lowliest manual tasks on their owners' farms and could be bought and sold like any chattel. Depending on the master, a slave's life was not always grim, and it was even possible in some cases for a slave to work his or her way to freedom.

On the next steps up the ladder were the *karls,* or free peasants, who hired out their services to landowners or other masters and sometimes owned small plots of land of their own. In this class, too, were artisans, peddlers, fishermen, shipwrights, small-time merchants, and mercenary soldiers who offered themselves to whatever leaders seemed most likely to succeed—often those second and third sons of landowning families, young men who were not in line to inherit the family estate and planned instead to win fame and fortune through expeditions into lands across the sea.

The owners of large tracts were members of the top rung of society, the aristocracy, and were known in large part as jarls, or earls. The more ambitious of these propertied chieftains aspired to be kings. They could achieve success by acquiring stashes of silver in one way or another and by attracting bands of warriors to extend their particular areas of influence. In any case, for members of this class to get what they wanted, they had to take major risks. Thus it was the aristocrats and their younger sons who were the true Vikings, and it was the essence of Vikinghood for a band of such men and their followers to journey to far countries and there perform heroic deeds and return in triumph with honor and rich prizes. And rich prizes meant the capacity to give gifts and attract yet more followers locally, tough young karls. This was the springboard to chieftainship and perhaps even to the throne of a petty kingdom.

From very early times, property owners of all classes—from freed slaves with small parcels of land to jarls with masses of real estate and even kings who claimed large areas for their own—came together in their various localities in a public assembly known as the thing. These things would select regional leaders and make laws regarding such matters as property, sheep stealing, and blood feuds. But there was an inner force in Viking life that was infinitely more influential than any external governing body could be and, indeed, informed every aspect of it.

In the Viking code of ethics, much depended on *drengeskapur*. The term implies a panoply of characteristics demanded of the whole of society and especially of those who would be heroes among their peers. Self-respect, honor, and reputation were necessary above all, and these could not exist without a firm foundation of loyalty to family and comrades. Conventions ruled everything in life—conventions about hospitality and the giving of gifts, about keeping oaths and avenging wrongs, about doing good deeds for the neighborhood such as building bridges and churches. Leaders of men must demonstrate courage, fortitude, fellowship, truthfulness, eloquence, and zest for life coupled with the ability to face death with an untroubled mind. All of these requirements, and countless others, were incorporated in the Old Norse poem *Havamal*, literally, "the speech of the high one," which includes the entire Viking-age code of conduct from simple little homilies to statements on the true meaning of eternal honor.

On the lesser end of the scale of importance, everyday guest etiquette must be observed: "He starts to stink," *Havamal* points out, "who outstays his welcome in a hall that is not his own." And if such a guest overindulges while lingering overlong with the ale, he is reminded that drinking and riding do not mix: "A more tedious burden than too much drink a traveler cannot carry." At the upper extreme of the code of conduct are *Havamal*'s concluding stanzas, addressing the linked themes of earning a good reputation in life and meeting death with honor in the course of a courageous deed: "Cattle die, kindred die, every man is mortal; but the

True Viking armor was Spartan in its simplicity, as shown by the 10th-century helmet at upper left and the remains of a chain-mail shirt below, discovered at Gjermundbu, Norway. This round-headed helmet is the only complete Viking-age helmet yet found, but it is known that Vikings also wore conical helmets into battle.

The Viking warrior's weapon of choice was the sword: simple, supple, sharp— and probably made in France, where the art of forging fine steel blades was highly refined. The hilts of these 11th-century swords, found in Finland, were covered with wood or some other material long since decayed. Javelins, spears, arrows, and the fearful Danish broadax were also part of the Viking arsenal.

good name never dies of one who has done well. Cattle die, kindred die, every man is mortal; but I know one thing that never dies, the glory of the great deed."

And thus the young men who lived by the code and were at home with the sea and ships turned their ambitions on foreign shores to perform bloody but glorious deeds for whatever plunder and profit they could obtain, earning the reputation of their choice but leaving an exceedingly bad name behind them. Even in early youth, Viking boys were expected and encouraged to show the bold spirit demanded by the *Havamal*. From the sagas comes the story of how Olaf, a warrior-king of Norway, sat his three little half-brothers on his lap and made horrible faces at them. The older two, Guttorm and Halfdan, were sorely frightened, but three-year-old Harald glowered right back and gave Olaf's mustache a mighty yank. Delighted, Olaf declared, "You will be revengeful one day, kinsman."

The next day, Harald further proved his Viking mettle when Olaf asked the three what they would most like to have in the world. Guttorm, stretching wide his tiny arms, opted for a field the size of the 10 largest neighboring farmsteads on which to grow grain. "There would be a great deal of grain there," the king allowed. "And

Halfdan?" Halfdan's wish was for miles and miles of cows, "so many that when they went down to the lake to drink they would be standing all the way round the lake, as closely packed as they could stand." "That would be setting up house on a large scale," the king observed. And what did little Harald want? "Warriors for my household," Harald said. "So many that they would eat up my brother Halfdan's cows at a single meal." Olaf laughed and said to the lad's mother, "You are bringing up a king." As it turned out, Olaf was right. The boy grew up to become King Harald Hardraade, who lost his life while invading England in 1066, shortly before the successful conquest by William of Normandy.

The term *king* was flexible. In early Viking times it was applied to any local chieftain who could both afford to maintain a following and claim its loyalty. In the long term, a man needed broader authority. He could never make it as a king if he did not have both income and honor. He required both to inspire his warriors. Honor decreed that he lead his own troops into battle, and honor thus determined that kings often died young. As recorded in the sagas, the Norwegian king Magnus Barefoot observed that "kings are made for honor, not for long life." Magnus proved the truth of his own remark: He was killed at age 30 during an expedition to Ireland in 1103.

If kings survived the battlefield, and if they succeeded in their self-appointed tasks, they lived exceedingly well. King Harald Bluetooth proclaimed his own fame on an ornamented rune-stone at Jelling in Jutland *(pages 82-83)*, probably erected not long before his death in 985: "King Harald had this monument raised in memory of his father Gorm and his mother Thyra. This was the Harald who won for himself all Denmark and Norway and made all the Danes Christians." Unification of the countries did not last long, and Christianity still had an uphill battle against the indigenous Viking gods, but Harald had made his name and carved out a genuine niche in history. He could not have done so had he not been the man his followers and close retainers wanted him to be—rich and generous.

Massive burial mounds haunt a wooded glade near the city of Horten, on Norway's Oslo Fjord. Excavations of the seven mounds in Borre reveal geological secrets: the wavy layer at the bottom of the trench seen at right, for instance, was once a beach. The mounds also offer proof of how important it was to the Norse to send their honored dead off in style.

Harald's palace, if it can even be called that, would have looked much like the long house of a wealthy farmer but more sumptuous and hung with tapestries depicting gods and heroes. At feast times the benches along the walls would be covered with cushions for the guests, and in front of them would be long tables decked with fine tableware—knives but no forks, spoons sometimes, washbasins, and goblets for beer, mead, and wine. The king would have a special seat in the middle of one of the main walls. A fire in the central hearth warmed and lit the scene, aided by oil lamps and candles.

Guests on all-male occasions such as royal feasts dressed in their finest garments and checked their weapons at the door. There was food and drink in abundance—fresh meat, boiled and roasted, fresh catches of fish, bread, dairy products, vegetables, fruits, nuts, and all manner of herbs and spices. The king and his guests ate and drank prodigiously. As they did so, musicians and jugglers entertained, and poets sang out verses that proclaimed the king's greatness.

The mark of a true leader was the staunch group of retainers he kept with him, whose loyalty was everlasting. These men lived on their lord's bounty, and in return for his generosity, they committed their lives to him. As a royal bard wrote with more than a touch of smugness: "One may see by their gear and their golden rings, they are comrades close to the king." It was always desirable to be close to a ruler, particularly one who understood the value of spectacular deeds and the virtue of being a figure larger than life. The same poet sang warmly of his liege's generosity and the life of his warriors: "They are favored with wealth and finest swordblades, with metal from Hunland and maids from the East; glad are they then when they guess battle's near, swift to leap up and lay hands to the oars"—thereupon to cheerfully, suicidally, cross the high seas to do their lord's bidding.

Even in death, bigness counted; it continued to awe and impress. At a place called Borre on the Oslo Fjord, not far from the spot where the Gokstad ship was unearthed, are several huge and majestic mounds. Once there were nine. One was excavated in 1853 by the indefatigable Nikolaysen, who found it to contain fragments of a ship buried in sand—the water permeable destroyer of all wooden remains. Another, in the course of time, fell in upon itself and disappeared. Now there are seven, and they are immense. Christian Keller, one of a team of Oslo archaeologists who began a new investigation of the giant mounds in 1988, conveyed their unusual size: "They are about 130 to 160 feet in diameter and about 23 feet high, which means that they contain some 141,000 cubic feet of mass—which is quite a lot. All along the coast of Norway we have single mounds of this size, but nothing compared to this as a group."

The dates of the scanty grave contents recovered from at least one of the mounds range from the beginning of the seventh century AD to the mid-ninth century, suggesting one early burial and another more than 200 years later. But according to Keller, it is more likely that secondary burials in this and other mounds would have been opportunistic. Probably the mounds were initially erected as the final resting places of pre-Viking royals and their entourages. Then along came pretenders, who either knew or assumed that the impressive mounds must be a prestigious burial center and tried to appropriate the site's power and esteem for themselves.

Yet the significance of the Borre mounds is not so much their sketchy history as their impact upon the coastal landscape of the Viking homeland. No doubt about it, they are big from any angle. But they are located right on the shoreline, on a slope below cultivated fields and forest lands, and from the road leading down the mountain slope they do not look particularly impressive. "Kind of timid," Christian Keller observed. But one day he went out in a boat and saw the mounds for the first time from the fjord.

"And when you see them from the waterside, you suddenly see them three times larger than they are. You get a kind of perspective distortion. They were built to be seen from the sea, not from the land. They look larger and more impressive from the water. So they functioned then and they function now as a kind of symbol for people passing on their way in and out of the fjord." The builders of the Borre mounds chose to decorate their piece of landscape according to their ideals: Be big, be bold, be noticed. Be a Viking, be three times larger than life. And the rest of you—beware!

SHIPS BENEATH THE WATER

What ship was that lying buried on the bottom of Denmark's Roskilde Fjord? Fishermen had known of its existence for many years, and legend held that the great 14th-century Danish queen Margrethe had scuttled it in order to block enemy passage into the waterway leading to the port city of Roskilde. Then, in 1956, two sports divers brought up an oak frame that they handed over to specialists at the Danish National Museum. Much to everyone's surprise, the wood, when it was analyzed, predated Margrethe's reign by some four centuries. The wreck could only be a Viking ship.

No underwater archaeology had ever been attempted in Denmark, and the museum decided to tackle the site as a learning experience. There seemed little reason to expect anything unusual; tides and ice were likely to have carried off much of the vessel over the years. Equipped with a small dinghy, a pontoon for supplies, rented diving gear, and a borrowed fire hose to wash the silt away, a five-member team commenced work in the fjord in 1957.

After removing the seaweed that covered the bed, the divers recorded on waterproof paper the dimensions of the 165-foot-long reef formed by the vessel. Next, they attacked the stones covering the ship and had not gone far when they exposed part of its keel. But now conditions worsened. Unless the hose was extended straight, it thrashed about. And the silt it stirred up turned the water so murky the divers sometimes had to wait for a current to carry the cloud away.

As more and more of the stones were removed, the ship's timbers appeared. And then the unexpected happened. A second keel came into view, sign of another vessel. But with the season over, a year would pass before the archaeologists could resume work. Little did they know that in the two seasons ahead they would uncover a mini Viking fleet—five ships in all, seen coming to light in the aerial photograph of the site above.

Returning to the site in 1958 with better equipment, the archaeologists were able to increase the pace of their investigations. Not only did they expose parts of the first ship and of the second one, but they also laid bare a portion of a third. For the archaeologists, the discovery of the last vessel was the high point of their work in the Roskilde Fjord. Its oak was so well preserved that they could see the ax marks left on the timbers by the boat builders. "To lie in that ship in the underwater silence and uncover one magnificent piece of timber after another was a unique experience," wrote one participant. "Each fragment was a little masterpiece of shipbuilding craftsmanship. We could study the planking, the frames, the keelson, the crossbeams, the knees. Everything was there." And best of all, the ship lay deep, which meant that the as-yet-unseen portions would probably be in good condition as well.

The third season, 1959, brought the discovery of two additional ships. Of the five that had been found, two proved to be warships (one, at 92 feet, the longest ever to be recovered), two were trading ships, and one was a small fishing boat. Laden with stones and pinned with stakes to the sandy floor of the tidal channel where the fjord was deepest, the vessels had been deliberately sunk in order to serve—as legend claimed that Queen Margrethe's ship had done—as an underwater line of defense against any enemy raiders. Although not much more than a yard deep over much of its breadth, the fjord contained tidal channels through which ships were able to navigate. It was in the deepest and therefore most navigable of these channels—sometime around the year 1000—that Roskilde's defenders had sunk their five vessels, establishing a blockage that would deter anyone without knowledge of the other channels from approaching the city.

During the three seasons, the divers brought up as much of the fragile ships' wood as they could but had to leave the thin planking behind, worried that in prying it loose they might damage it. Each waterlogged piece was measured, numbered, and wrapped in plastic to keep it from drying out. But if the ships were to be reconstructed, as was the archaeologists' hope, it would be necessary to salvage what still remained of the hulls on the fjord's bottom. An ingenious plan was eventually devised. In the spring of 1962, sheet piling was driven into the channel bed to form a cofferdam so that the water could be pumped from the site. An observation platform with a jetty was constructed on one side of the dam, and work sheds were erected on posts in the water. The delicate task of recovery could now begin.

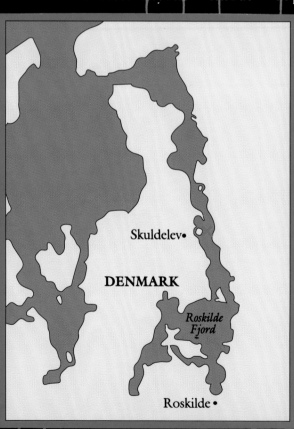

The five scuttled vessels blocked the Peberrenden, one of the most important navigational channels in the Roskilde Fjord, which leads from the North Sea to Roskilde. The wrecks lay near the harbor town of Skuldelev, 12½ miles north of the city.

Skuldelev•

DENMARK

Roskilde Fjord

Roskilde •

Gold traces the outlines of the five ships at the bottom of the Roskilde Fjord and shows how they overlapped. Surrounding the wrecks is the coffer-dam that held back the water while archaeologists worked on the drained site. The artificial island encompassed more than 17,000 feet.

Jetties lead to the drained area, which was supplied and serviced by boat. On an islet close to the mainland stood a house and a shed where archaeologists could store equipment.

SALVAGING THE WRECKS FROM THE MUCK

During the first three seasons' of their diving expeditions, the archaeologists had raised some of the larger, better-preserved lengths of timber. But the remaining pieces, which they had covered up again with stones, remained at the bottom of the fjord until the cofferdam could be built around the site.

In 1962, using two large electric pumps on a pontoon moored inside the dam, the archaeologists began carefully draining the water. The danger, as the water flowed away, was that the stones would shift and crush the wood. In order to prevent this, the draining was done gradually, a few inches a day.

Once the ships appeared above the surface, groups of students, supervised by more experienced hands, cleared the vessels of their stony blankets. Lying facedown on movable catwalks that were suspended above the wreckage, the workers used jets of water from a network of hoses to loosen the rocks, which were then carried in buckets to waiting wheelbarrows.

In order to reduce the chance of anything falling from the catwalk onto the exposed timber and damaging it, the wheelbarrows were kept at the periphery of the excavation and metal implements were forbidden. The buckets used were made of plastic, as were the toy shovels and kitchen scrapers the excavators employed when their bare hands were not sufficient to clear away the debris.

Another danger—that the timber would dry out and possibly warp or crack—was averted by the use of 19 sprinklers, which kept the wood continually damp but obliged the workers to wear rain gear even on the sunniest of days.

In a little more than two months, all the ships had been uncovered. The archaeologists kept a detailed record of each vessel—its characteristics, construction, degree of preservation. After photographing sections with a special three-dimensional camera, they attached numbered tags to every part, indicating the vessel to which it belonged and its position relative to the main members of the ship. Only then could they transport the pieces to the workshop, where conservation efforts could get underway. All told some 50,000 fragments were rescued and moved.

Draped on a catwalk above the artificial island, a student volunteer removes a rock from the small trading ship, the first vessel found, while a companion scoops mud into plastic buckets, using bare hands as trowels. Cold, damp weather complicated the process, and many of the workers came down with flu.

Two large pumps like this one were used to remove water from the dam. During the excavation, smaller pumps kept the water at the proper level. But the 1962 season was particularly stormy, and wind-driven water threatened to flow over the dam and resubmerge the site.

Garden sprinklers keep the trading vessel's exposed timbers damp. Each location had two sprinklers; if one of them broke down, the other ensured that the timbers would not dry out and shrink.

Two of the ships uncovered evoked the Vikings' trading, rather than raiding, past. And this stirred the Danish archaeologists. They knew well that the world tends to think of their ancestors as fierce seaborne warriors. But here, in these wrecks, was tangible evidence of the Vikings' other, much greater role as peaceful traders who "brought," in the words of one of the archaeologists, "the greatest and most lasting wealth to the North."

One of two vessels was a *knorr*, a ship large enough and heavy enough to negotiate the Atlantic Ocean—probably the type that conveyed Viking settlers, with their household goods and livestock, to Iceland and Greenland. The other was a relatively lightweight craft thought to be typical of vessels the Vikings used to plow the Baltic and North seas.

Both ships had been specifi-cally designed for commercial purposes. Higher on the sides and wider than sleek fighting vessels, they had midship holds; leather tarpaulins stretched over these would have kept the cargo from getting soaked. The two vessels had obviously seen heavy duty over the years; they showed a great deal of wear and tear.

Though small, the lighter of the two ships—the one that had so fascinated the divers when they first came upon it—proved to be the more significant find; indeed, it was the most exciting discovery of all. Unlike the other vessels in the fjord, which had been flattened into formlessness by the weight of the stones that pinned them to the channel bed, this one largely held

its shape. Moreover, 75 percent of its original 44-foot length was intact. The stern had long since disappeared, but the gracefully curving prow, hewn from a single piece of oak, had survived its thousand-year submersion. It culminated in a point, befitting a plain trading ship (a dragon's head would have graced a chieftain's vessel). And since no other Viking ship had ever been found with its prow entirely whole, the discovery called for a celebration—someone went over to the mainland and came back with red wine to toast the achievement.

Examination of the vessel's sides revealed seven square oar holes, only four of which actually showed signs of wear. This suggested to the archaeologists that the crew must have numbered from four to six men. Since the ship apparently had a mast, it had probably been propelled more by wind than muscle power.

A worker lays bare the tip of the prow of the little trading vessel, which still lies buried in its bed of sand, shells, and stones. The wreck lay the deepest of the five ships in the channel, which partially accounted for its high state of preservation.

The prow—carved from a single piece of oak—stands revealed after careful removal of the material that surrounded it. Regarded by the archaeologists as a major find, it was promptly wrapped in plastic to prevent it from deteriorating and became the core piece from which the ship was eventually reconstructed.

Pressed into the sandy bottom of the fjord, the trading ship displays its seafaring form. It was found under another ship at the southern end of the channel.

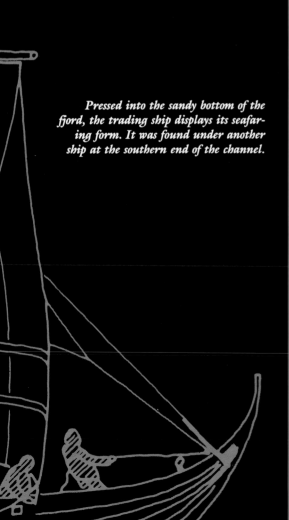

Filling 1,500 tightly sealed plastic bags, the fragile ship timbers and fragments were conveyed on cushioning plastic foam by truck to the conservation laboratory of the National Museum at Brede, near Copenhagen. But even though the pieces had been sprayed with water before they were sealed in the airtight bags, some were threatening to crack. So until they could be worked on, they were immersed—still swathed in plastic—in large water tanks.

When the timber finally emerged from its plastic cocoons, it underwent a thorough but gentle washing that removed any remaining silt. One such bath exposed a simple etched design on a plank from the smaller of the warships, the only decorative element to turn up on any of the vessels.

Like pieces in a jigsaw puzzle, the fragments were then temporarily reassembled. A plate of glass covered with a transparent plastic film was laid on a metal support over each length, enabling a draftsman to trace every detail, down to the nail holes. These drawings provided a standard against which any reduction in size brought about during the conservation process could later be gauged.

To strengthen and further preserve the wood—which if untreated would soon have begun to decompose—a waxy substance called glycol was used. The planks and fragments were affixed to supports of perforated masonite, then lowered into tanks filled with a circulating solution of glycol and water. It took six months to two years, depending upon the kind of wood, for the glycol to penetrate the cells of each piece and stabilize it.

Now, at last, the ships could be reconstructed from the treated wood. But this involved more than joining pieces together. Since much of the wood had been deformed by its centuries-long sojourn in the water, various parts had to be reshaped before they could be reassembled. It was a process of trial and error, demanding the special feel of a professional shipwright, and one was hired.

Work began on the large cargo ship, or knorr. Brittle as a result of the glycol treatment, the vessel's keel was gently heated in order to make it more malleable; then it was placed in a press to restore its curvature. Fragments of plank were shaped in a mold and glued and tacked together. Then, supported and reinforced by a system of rails, the hull was rebuilt from the surviving fragments.

After spraying each piece of wood, a worker heat-seals the numbered plastic bags in which the timbers were sent to the conservation laboratory.

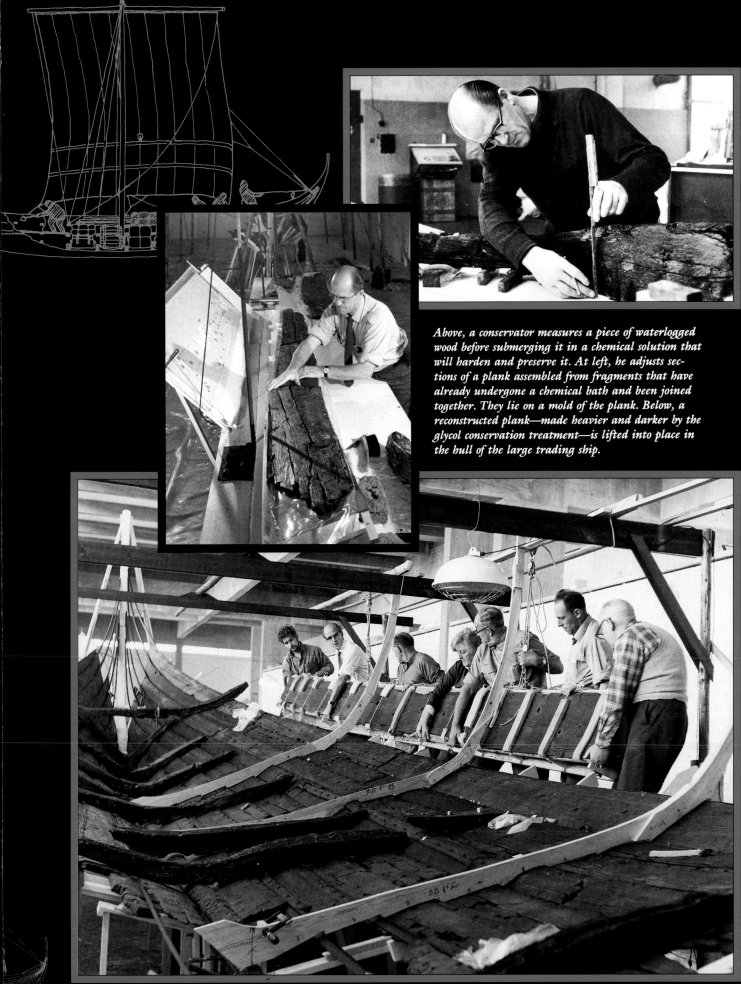

Above, a conservator measures a piece of waterlogged wood before submerging it in a chemical solution that will harden and preserve it. At left, he adjusts sections of a plank assembled from fragments that have already undergone a chemical bath and been joined together. They lie on a mold of the plank. Below, a reconstructed plank—made heavier and darker by the glycol conservation treatment—is lifted into place in the hull of the large trading ship.

WHOLE AGAIN IN THE VIKING SHIP MUSEUM

As news spread of the discoveries in the Roskilde Fjord, several Danish cities indicated interest in providing a final home for the ships. Roskilde won out, and plans began to be developed for a steel and glass structure to house the vessels. But for a while, it looked to the scientists as though there might not be any reconstructed ships to display there.

During the initial experimental stage of the glycol treatment, several pieces of the wood—as evidenced by the drawings of them made earlier—had shrunk in treatment. The scientists now attempted to find out why it had happened. The glycol, they learned, had penetrated the outer layers of the oak easily enough but not the heartwood. Discouraged, they sought to remove the glycol. They placed the oak in baths of hot and cold water; fortunately, the heat dissolved the glycol, the water filled the wood cells, and the wood plumped out again.

Through what one of the participants referred to as "a charming blend of al-chemy and science," the conservation process was reexamined and refined. A substance called butanol, a form of alcohol, was substituted for the water—and it worked. The butanol distributed the glycol throughout the oak, firming the wood without shrinking it. At last, the conservators could think about the task of putting the ships back together again.

But there was another problem. One of the warships had turned out to be the longest one ever discovered—a whole lot longer than the plans for the museum allowed. Nothing would do then but to have these revised, and the room in which the vessels were to be housed was expanded.

The ships' pieces were mounted on metal frames, and slowly the vessels took shape. No effort was made to fill in the missing parts. The two trading ships were given place of honor in front of a large glass wall that faced out onto the fjord, against whose waters they were dramatically silhouetted.

As is clear even in the partial reconstructions, these were ships that had been built by people attuned to both form and function. Working with primitive tools and no knowledge of calculus, they had managed to create vessels that were eminently seaworthy and beautiful as well. Today, of course, they are a tribute not just to the Viking shipbuilders' art and the Viking shipbuilders' past but also to the modern scientific ingenuity that saved them from their rock-filled graves in the Roskilde Fjord.

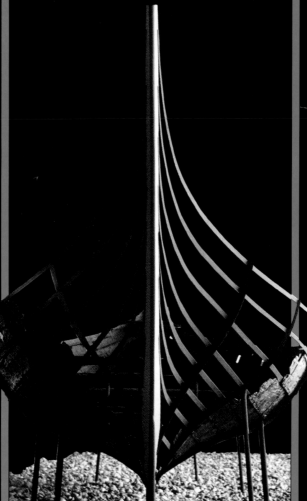

Even with its stern missing, the restored small trading vessel displays the proud bearing of a Viking ship and a survivor.

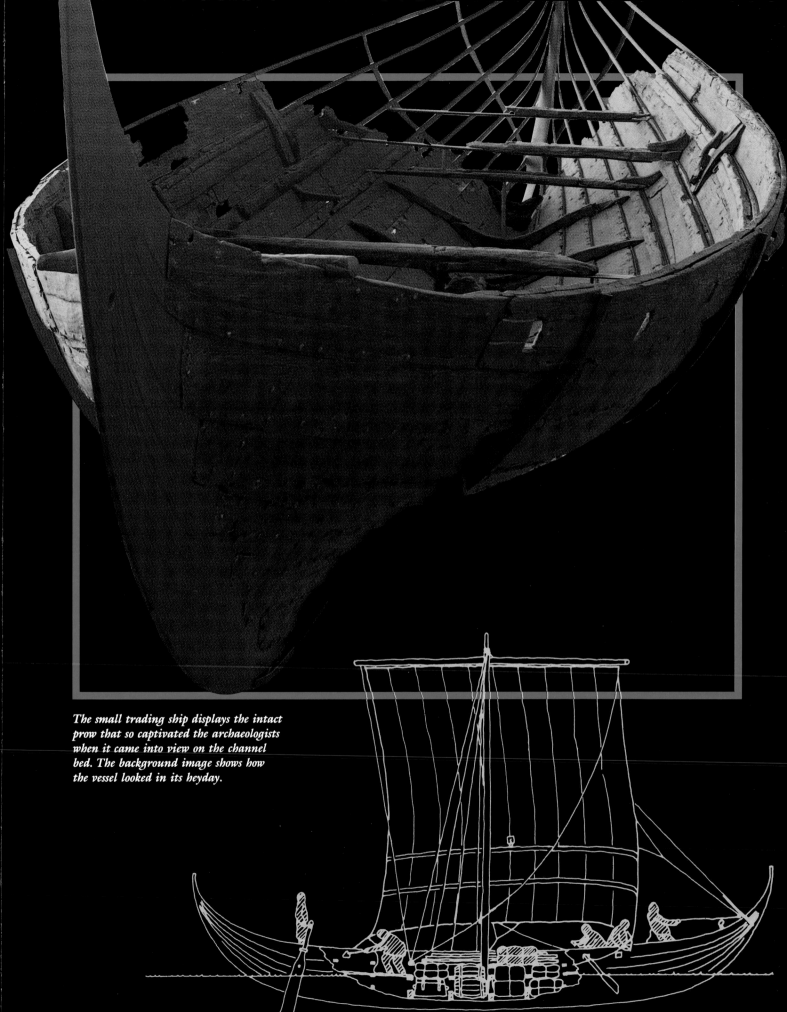

The small trading ship displays the intact prow that so captivated the archaeologists when it came into view on the channel bed. The background image shows how the vessel looked in its heyday.

THE BOUNDLESS QUEST FOR WEALTH AND GLORY

he Viking market town of Birka had slumbered forgotten beneath the meadows of Sweden's Björkö Island, about 19 miles from Stockholm, for nearly a millennium. Only a blackened swath of earth—the decomposed debris of centuries of human habitation—marked the site of the once-bustling settlement. It was not this darkened blot, however, that first drew the attention of the Swedish naturalist Hjalmar Stolpe in the fall of 1871 but the reports of pieces of handworked amber, which had been found beneath the waters off Björkö's coast. Stolpe knew that amber had been prized as ornaments for barter in Viking-age Europe. The island, with its sheltered access to the sea, seemed the perfect place for a trading community.

Stolpe's excavations, conducted between 1872 and 1895, revealed a ninth-century town—a 30-acre labyrinth of wattle and daub dwellings, shops, and smithies—surrounded by earthen ramparts. Behind the ruins of the settlement, which once housed perhaps 500 to 1,000 inhabitants, clustered several large cemeteries. Intermingled with the cremation mounds of the island dwellers were numerous graves of merchants—some belonging to overseas traders—filled with rich burial goods. Here, in these far-northern cemeteries, were remnants of silks and thick brocades from Byzantium and still finer imperial silks from China; tiny glass gaming pieces thought to have

Bronze scales, precise, portable, and vital to the Viking trader, were used to measure the weight of precious metals, such as these silver Arabic coins received in exchange for Viking goods.

come from Charlemagne's Frankish empire and glass goblets and flasks from the Rhineland. In one grave, the remains of an embroidered jacket and fur hat fringed with silver tassels adorned a man's body. At his side was a hammer-ax and a set of the bronze balances used for weighing out silver, perhaps indicating that in life he had pursued the dual professions of warrior and trader. In other graves were found an amethyst ring from the Caspian Sea incised with Arabic script, leather pieces from Persian belts embellished with metal studs, and scraps of fine woolen cloth, dyed blue, from Frisia on the northwest coast of the European continent. Scattered throughout the graves were coins, including some from Arab lands, a major source of Viking silver.

Birka's ecclectic riches reflect the vitality and breadth of the Vikings' 9th- and 10th-century outreach, which extended west and east to the limits of the world then known to Europeans. Beginning around AD 800, Norse traders, raiders, and adventurers sailed from northern lands in their longships toward the continents of Europe, Africa, and Asia. A thin but tantalizing trail of archaeological evidence chronicles more than a century of plunder and settlement by Danes and Norwegians throughout the British Isles, the Low Countries, France, Spain, Morocco, and Italy. Now and again, the odd weapon—a double-edged sword with an extremely rare gold-inlaid hilt, for instance, or a silver-ornamented spear—washes free from a riverbank where it has lain these thousand years. In France, the decades-long visitation of the Norsemen is recalled by the fading image of a Viking ship etched into a cliff along the Seine. To the east, the Swedes' progress across the Baltic and down the great rivers of Russia to Byzantium and the Arab caliphate is marked every so often by long-lost fort cities, Viking burials, and isolated hoards of silver coins.

According to Nordic archaeologists, a hoard is normally defined as several objects made of precious metal that were deliberately hidden in the ground. In the absence of banks, Vikings used the soil of their homesteads as a sort of safe-deposit box. Only the owner

A rampart of earth and stone surrounds the site of the vanished trading center of Birka, located on a small island in central Sweden. The town's great success as a marketplace hinged on its secure location and the so-called Law of Birka, which offered equal protection under the law for both Viking and foreigner.

knew his treasure's exact location, which must have given him a feeling of security when he went off a-Viking. But the risks that accompanied such forays are amply demonstrated by the more than 1,000 Viking-age hoards found in modern times whose owners never returned to dig them up.

Although such depositories show that the Norsemen brought back quantities of precious metal to Scandinavia, scant physical traces remain of their presence abroad. Yet, like a shock wave, they radiated outward from their lands, rearranging—through trade, conquest, and settlement—the underpinnings of European civilization. In Normandy and Kiev, Norse colonists sowed great dynasties that would eventually give rise to the empires of Britain and Russia.

For nearly 1,000 years prior to the great outpouring of around AD 800, ships had sporadically sortied from Scandinavian waters in search of markets, loot, and land on the fringes of the Baltic and North Atlantic. Historians have debated why this trickle of adventurers suddenly swelled to a torrent. If the Vikings are to be believed, the cause—as confided on their rune-stones —was, of course, the lure of honor and treasure, especially silver, of which they had none themselves. By the ninth century, western Europe's coastal markets posed temptation indeed, overflowing with luxurious wares, as the contents of many Swedish boat graves of that time affirm.

Snow highlights the burial mounds that fill the woods outside the walls of Birka. This cemetery, known as Hemlanden, or the Homelands, contains some 1,600 graves and is one of the largest from the Viking age in Sweden. Rich grave goods from many parts of the world reveal 10th-century Birka as quite cosmopolitan.

Meanwhile, silver from the Arab caliphate made its first appearance in the lands east of the Baltic, whetting the greed of Viking fur traders working the Gulf of Finland. Eventually, silver—acquired through trade, pillage, or payoffs—fueled the whole Scandinavian economy. In fact, a cutoff in the flow of Arab silver into Sweden around AD 970 may have led to Birka's abrupt demise as a commercial hub. But other sources of the precious metal were found, and other trading centers sprang up to handle the flow of goods to and from the Viking lands.

None of this, however, could have occurred without major advances in Viking shipbuilding technology. Early Norse ships depended almost exclusively on oar power to propel them down the rivers and along the coasts. Though light in the water and easy to beach, they could carry only small payloads and travel limited distances. But images carved in stone dating from the beginning of the eighth century and found on the island of Gotland show masted merchant vessels running before the wind, square sails billowing. Such ships could cover up to 120 miles a day and, with their shallow draft, land just about anywhere.

By the first decade of the ninth century, an armada of these square-riggers regularly menaced western Europe, tacking up and down the coastline, looking for a breach in the defense chain. Under Charlemagne, who is said to have harbored a dread of Viking attack, the bulwark held. The empire did not fare so well, however, once Charlemagne's successors took over. His grandsons, Charles the Bald, Louis the German, and Lothar, fell to bickering and allowed the well-knit fabric of Charlemagne's defenses to fray. In 834 a flotilla of Danish ships penetrated inland along an arm of the Rhine to the great Frisian trading center of Dorestad.

Not only was Dorestad among the richest markets in all of western Europe—and a prime trading partner of Birka—it also boasted a mint where silver deniers, or Frisian pennies, were stamped. The Viking raiders made straight for the emporium, passing unmolested through the town's stockaded wall. After sacking the market stalls and looting the mint, they rounded up captives—either for ransom or as slaves—and put the town to torch, leaving behind a grisly trail of dead and dying.

Thereafter, pillaging Dorestad became almost routine. The Vikings returned yearly until 837 and then sporadically for a generation. Yet for all they took away, they left little behind of their own presence. Only a gold armband and finger ring—valuables loosed, perhaps, from a Dane's purse during one of the many assaults—remained in Dorestad's soil.

From spring through autumn, sea kings and pirates fell upon the poorly defended coastal margins of western Europe, the Seine and Loire valleys, and the provinces of Brittany and Aquitaine. The annals of the monastery of St.-Wandrille de Fontenelle in the Neustria region of France recall Viking barbarity:

A Rhenish ceramic pitcher decorated with geometric motifs and a funnel-shaped glass drinking vessel represent widespread wine-related trade during the Viking age. Many such jugs and beakers, which probably accompanied casks of wine from the Rhineland, came to light in Birka.

A finely carved soapstone mold for an ornamental pin in the shape of a dragon mimics in miniature the figureheads of Viking ships. The mold, found at Birka and illustrative of craftwork produced there, also includes a form for making a flat-headed pin with which to affix a metal brooch like the one shown here.

"At dawn on May 13, 841, the monks watched with stupefaction" as the dragon ships glided silently up the Seine. At Rouen, the Scandinavians paused for two days of plunder and burning and then retraced their path, "amusing themselves by sacking churches and abbeys," as the annals put it, carrying away jeweled crucifixes, illuminated manuscripts, and golden altar pieces. The roads were soon overrun with monks and townspeople fleeing before the invaders' sturdy axes, swords, and spears.

The raw spirit of adventurism and avarice soon drove the Norsemen south along the French coast to the Moorish lands of the Iberian Peninsula and North Africa. In 844 a Viking fleet of 100 ships or so set sail from Aquitaine to the north of Spain, where it terrorized the Christian communities at Gijón and La Coruña. Moving south, the Norsemen spent a fortnight raiding Lisbon, Cádiz, and Morocco's Atlantic coast. Then, they turned inland up the Guadalquivir River to Seville, major port of the Spanish Moors, who had conquered most of Spain by 711. The invaders laid the city to waste, stripping its mosques of their finery, slaying the men, and carrying off the women as spoils.

The Moors struck back hard, catapulting balls of flaming naphtha at the Norse fleet and sinking 30 of the invaders' ships. The emir Abd al-Rahman II hanged scores of Vikings from Seville's date palms. As a final gesture, he sent the heads of a Viking chieftain and 200 of his warriors to his Moorish ally in Morocco. Now desperate, the Viking holdouts ransomed their Muslim captives for food, clothing, and safe passage and would not venture into the land of the Moors again for nearly 15 years.

In 859 the veteran Danish pirate Bjorn Ironside returned to Iberia with a fleet of 62 dragon ships. Heading through the Strait of Gibraltar, he and his men plundered the riches of Algeciras's grand mosque and then swept northern Morocco, rounding up slaves for future sale. From there the raiders harried the southern coast of France and traveled down the Italian boot to the Arno River, sacking Pisa, Luna, and Fiesole. Arab sources claim the Danes ultimately reached as far as Greece and Egypt. But meager evidence exists for these southern exploits—only silver coins, minted in Moorish Spain and North Africa, found in Viking-age hoards in Norway.

Meanwhile, elsewhere in Europe the Viking raiders com-

TRAPPED SUNSHINE, GIFT FROM THE SEA

The routes southward taken by Viking merchants had been followed for centuries before by northern traders, spurred by the craving of Europeans for a peculiarly Baltic substance—luminous, golden amber. Ancient Romans had paid more for a small amber figure than for a slave, and the Roman emperor Nero once purchased 13,000 pounds of the raw material. Color increased its value; most amber comes in variants of yellow, red, or brown, but some 250 different shades have been noted, including rare blue and green hues.

Amber is fossilized resin, which was secreted millions of years ago by coniferous trees in forests that later were submerged by encroaching seas. Fist-sized lumps collected on the shores of the southern Baltic and the North Sea after being dislodged by currents from underwater sources. In some areas, a few acres of beach yielded thousands of pounds.

When polished to a satiny texture, a piece glows like sunshine, and not surprisingly amber was associated with sun worship. Amber was also considered magical and therapeutic because of its unusual properties. Extremely light in weight, it seems to retain warmth. When rubbed, it builds up a charge of static electricity. The Greeks called it *elektron,* from which the word *electric* is derived. Romans wore amber necklaces to help cure a sore throat or a toothache.

The amber trade was a staple of the Viking economy. Rough amber was brought to workshops that were located in trading centers such as Wolin, Hedeby, Birka, Ribe, York, and Dublin. There it was carved, drilled, and polished into rounded and multifaceted beads for necklaces and rosaries as well as into pendants and charms in the form of small animals, cultic symbols, and gods such as Frey, seen below, in the form of a Danish gaming piece, clutching his beard.

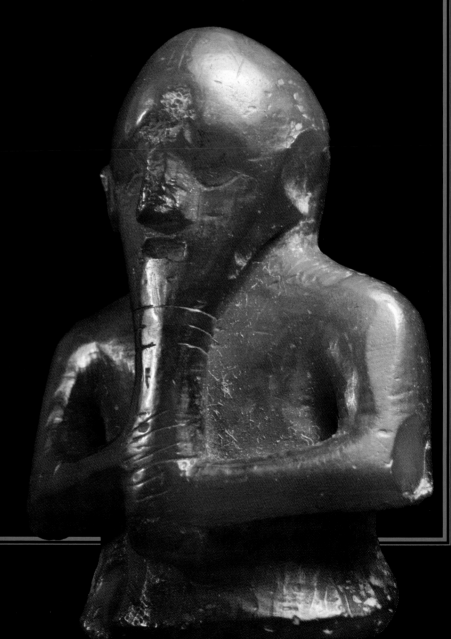

menced an intensified phase of well-coordinated, sustained assaults. No longer did they return to Scandinavia during winter to trap silver fox or sire more sons. To go a-Viking had become a year-round occupation, too lucrative to relegate to fair-weather months alone. Viking bands took to beaching their boats at the mouths of rivers along Europe's western and northern coasts, some using islands as their long-term abodes. In 1906 the French archaeologist Paul du Chatellier found a Viking burial mound on the Île de Groix near the mouth of the Loire River. Centuries of erosion had eaten away at the mound's base, revealing a burned area strewn with 800 boat rivets, 200 nails, and 15 European shield bosses. Small ornaments, such as stocking buckles and beads of silver, littered the site. Nearby lay the charred fragments of a saddle, a drinking horn, dice, gaming pieces, and a Frankish sword. From this evidence, du Chatellier surmised that a Norwegian chieftain had been cremated with his belongings in a 40-foot oaken boat sometime in the early 10th century. The Île de Groix, located off the south coast of Brittany astride the great maritime trade route, would have made an ideal raiders' den.

Just 60 miles southeast of the Île de Groix lies Noirmoutier, the first of the Vikings' island homes. According to contemporary chronicles, Count Lambert, a Frankish nobleman, after trying unsuccessfully to capture the old Roman walled town of Nantes, sent an emissary to a squadron of 67 Viking ships that was stalled in the Loire's estuary. The count offered to pilot the longships through the maze of sand flats to the rich towns upstream—if they would help him to seize Nantes on the way.

The Norsemen gladly obliged. On June 24, 842, a holy feast day marking the birth of John the Baptist, the town's residents were too absorbed in their merrymaking to notice the stealthy approach of the Viking ships. With unconscionable savagery, Lambert's Viking mercenaries fell upon the celebrants and hacked them to pieces. The invaders slew the bishop at the altar of his own cathedral and then set the bell tower aflame. At dusk, they rowed their heavily laden ships back down the Loire toward the sea. Just beyond the river's mouth, the Vikings set up camp on Noirmoutier. The community of monks that had once overseen the island's thriving trade in salt and wine had fled under a prior attack. The raiders thus had the fair isle all to themselves and settled in for the winter—as if, bemoaned one chronicler, "they meant to stay for ever."

The Seine estuary was dotted with islets where, from the

mid-840s on, Vikings beached their craft, restocked their larders, and plotted their next exploit. No doubt it was another such island that in 845 hosted the infamous raider Ragnar and his Danish flotilla of 120 ships on their way to Paris in 845.

By mid-March, with Ragnar's fleet approaching, Charles the Bald, king of the West Franks since 843, quickly conscripted an army and unwisely divided it in two to guard both banks of the Seine. But the Vikings trounced the inept monarch's smaller force, taking 111 prisoners. Then, as the second group watched in horror, Ragnar staged the riverside sacrifice of his Frankish captives, hanging them on makeshift gallows in honor of Odin, Norse god of battle. Ragnar met with no more resistance. On March 28, Easter Sunday, he ravaged Paris. To induce the Danes to leave, Charles offered them the awesome sum of 7,000 pounds of silver. They accepted. So it was that Ragnar, clutching a bar taken from the Paris city gate as a souvenir, departed the region, ships overflowing with Frankish silver.

The hefty ransom paid to Ragnar was the first of many so-called Danegelds, or Danish money, surrendered to Vikings over the coming years by the fiefdoms of western Europe to bring respite from the otherwise endless barrage of assaults. During the 9th and 10th centuries, the Franks paid at least 15 such Danegelds to the Norse, totaling well over 40,000 pounds of silver and 600 pounds of gold. And between the end of the 10th century and the beginning of the 11th, the English contributed an even bigger amount—over 150,000 pounds of silver. In Scandinavian hands, the metal was often melted down and made into armbands and neck rings worn by both men and women as an outward sign of their wealth.

In 1834 a landowner in Hon, Norway, 35 miles southwest of Oslo, discovered a 5½-pound stash of gold that archaeologists believe may have once been part of a Viking ransom. Dubbed the Hon hoard, it included an exquisite brooch filigreed with vines and leaves, 20 ornamental Frankish coins, two neckbands, and numerous bracelets. Much of the work is characteristic of a goldsmith from Reims. Dates on the coins indicate the hoard was buried sometime around 860—a year in which Frankish ledgers show the payment of a 5,000-pound Danegeld to Norse raiders.

In the long run, Danegelds did little to alleviate the growing Viking threat. By 862 even Charles the Bald was finding the expedient of ransom a poor safeguard. The Nordmanni, as the Franks called the

SAFE HAVENS IN TIMES OF TROUBLE

The Vikings frequently did to each other what they did unto others: They seized the gold and silver their compatriots brought home from overseas raids. Because no one's booty was ever quite safe, they often buried it in secret on family homesteads. For those who died protecting such wealth, their forgotten troves, retrieved in more recent eras, tell of their plight.

Throughout parts of Sweden, Norway, and Finland, ruins exist of more than a thousand hilltop forts—already old in Viking times—to which locals retreated when in peril. Such rich trading centers as Sweden's Birka and Denmark's Hedeby built formidable earthworks around their commercial districts. At Hedeby, the earthen rampart—up to 40 feet high and encompassing 60 acres—still dominates the landscape. In the ninth century, King Godfred constructed a chain of earthworks connected by natural barriers that stretched across the narrow base of the Jutland Peninsula—to ward off looters from the south. Forts could also serve as staging areas for foreign raids or as domestic garrisons. King Harald Bluetooth built several, including Fyrkat at right, throughout Denmark to house his mercenary soldiers and act as centers of royal adminstration.

One of 19 "ring-forts" on the Baltic island Öland, the village of Eketorp (above), inhabited off and on between 300 and 1200, has been excavated and partly reconstructed to reflect its appearance between 400 and 700.

Typical of royal Danish forts, Fyrkat's symmetrical rampart of compacted earth and stone faced with heavy timbers contained four gates. The interior (diagram, below) was divided into quadrants by two wood-planked streets. From postholes and traces of hearths, archaeologists have determined that large wooden buildings—consisting of dwellings, workshops, stables, and barns—precisely filled each quadrant.

Vikings, continued to pillage Frisia and the West Frankish Kingdom with impunity. "The number of ships increases, the endless flood of Vikings never ceases to grow bigger," wrote the monk Ermentarius in the 860s. "Everywhere Christ's people are the victims of massacre, burning, and plunder." But such harassment was only a prelude to the savage onslaught of the 880s. In 877 Charles the Bald died, and over the next 11 years, the West Frankish Kingdom had five different rulers. For the Vikings, such confusion proved an irresistible lure: From beachheads between Calais and Boulogne, they fanned out over the continent, wreaking havoc as they went. In 885, seeking passage to the rich valley of the Marne beyond Paris, the Danes again laid siege to the city—this time for an entire year. Finally, the nominal emperor of the Franks, Charles the Fat, bought off the offensive with a Danegeld of 700 pounds and the promise of unhampered looting in Charles's rebellious province of Burgundy.

Yet the Vikings were no longer content with simple plunder. They now expropriated villages, driving away residents and setting up housekeeping. Many brought their Scandinavian wives along; a woman's grave at Pîtres that yielded two Norse tortoise brooches may be the final resting place of one. Most of these settlements were short-lived—casualties of the shifting alliances and recurrent conquests of the age. Only one, the Viking fiefdom of Normandy—literally, the Land of the Northmen—would endure. Its singular destiny was rooted in the uncommon wit of a Norse chieftain known as Hrolf the Walker, a man so large no horse could hold him.

Hrolf's early years are shrouded in mystery; it is not even known whether, as legend says, he was Norwegian, since he seems to have commanded an army of Danes. By the early 10th century the fog of history had thinned sufficiently to place him in the Frankish province of Neustria, where he and his followers are said to have overrun and occupied the rich bottom lands of the Seine. Little plunder was left in this harried domain, but there were lush meadows and orchards heavy with fruit. The Vikings resolved to stay. Unable to evict the Norsemen, Charles the Bald's grandson Charles the Simple agreed to cede the broad valley of the lower Seine to Hrolf—and with it the title count of Rouen—in exchange for his fealty and conversion to Christianity. In 911 the two formalized the treaty at St.-Clair-sur-Epte, on a tributary of the Seine between Paris and Rouen. The bargain served both well; Hrolf—ever-after known as Rollo—won legitimacy and land to rule, while Charles gained a fierce ally in

Exquisite neck rings, armbands, and filigreed pendants fashioned from gold, silver, and beads make up the 5½-pound Norwegian cache of loot known as the Hon hoard. The treasure, undoubtedly procured through Viking raid or ransom, contains items of Frankish, Anglo-Saxon, Byzantine, and Scandinavian origin.

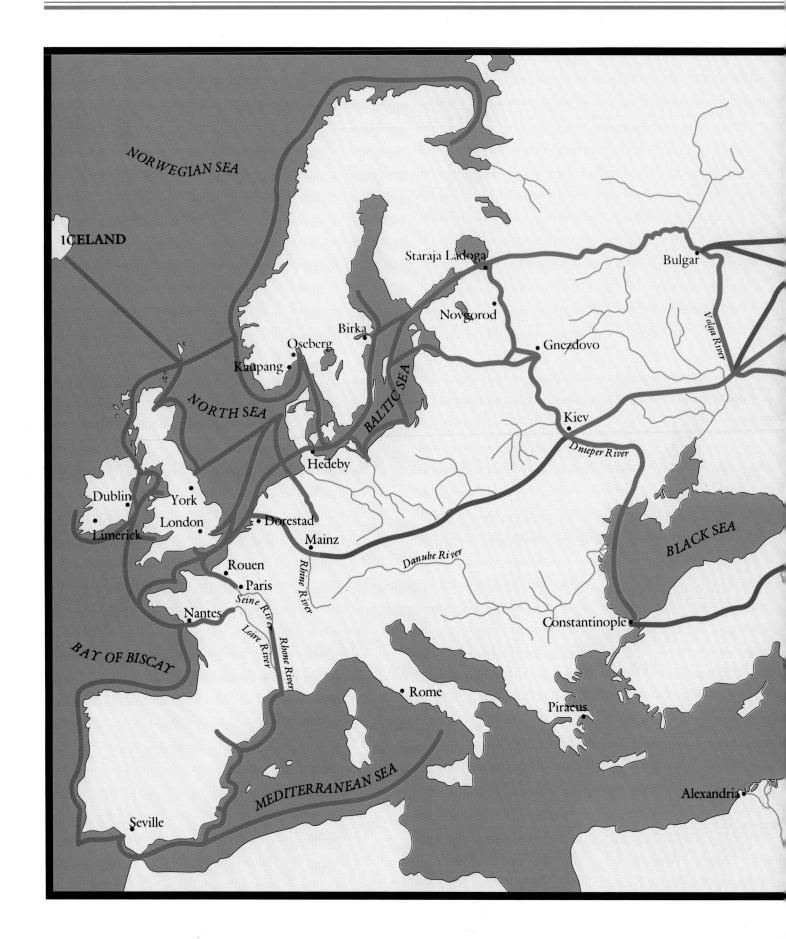

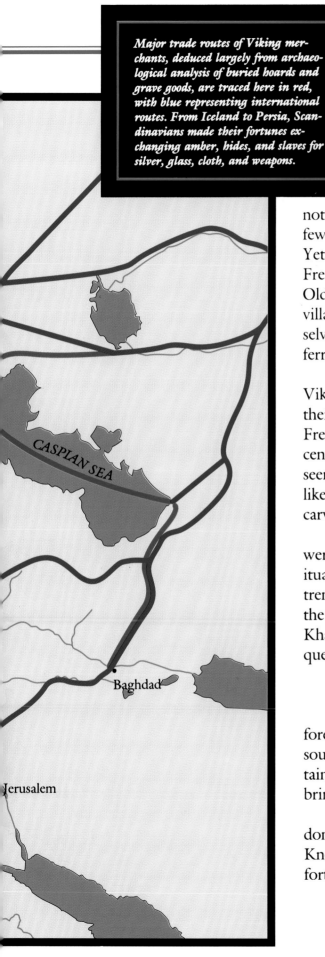

Major trade routes of Viking merchants, deduced largely from archaeological analysis of buried hoards and grave goods, are traced here in red, with blue representing international routes. From Iceland to Persia, Scandinavians made their fortunes exchanging amber, hides, and slaves for silver, glass, cloth, and weapons.

CASPIAN SEA

Baghdad

Jerusalem

fending off insurgent nobles and other Viking raiders.

By 912 Rollo and his men had cast aside their pagan amulets and nominally embraced Christianity. Rollo retained at least one Viking institution, however, that of *more danico*—"the Danish custom"—polygamy. Still, the women Rollo's men took to wife were French—not Scandinavian—who raised French-speaking children. Within a few generations, few speakers of Old Norse remained in Normandy. Yet even today, echoes of this forgotten language resound in Norman French: The highest point of any town is always *hogue*, from *haugr*, Old Norse for hill; and the thicket of trees at the center of an inland village is the *londe*, from *lundr*, or grove. Many town names themselves, such as Quettehou and Houlgate, are the same as those conferred by their Viking founders a thousand years before.

Aside from such linguistic remnants, little evidence of the Vikings remains in Normandy. In time, the Normans lost touch with their ancestral homeland, becoming—to all intents and purposes—Frenchmen. But they remained Norse in spirit. During the 11th century, Normandy rose to be the most formidable European state seen since the fall of Rome. Through six generations, Rollo's heirs, like their Viking forebears, sallied from their Norman stronghold to carve out kingdoms in Britain, Italy, and Sicily.

And, as with Rollo's original band, these latter-day Norse were assimilated into the cultures they conquered. Theirs was a spiritual legacy—a gift of hardihood, daring, and leadership that sparked tremendous change in the European political order. To the east, into the lands of taiga and steppe inhabited by the Slavs, Bulgars, and Khazars, the Vikings would also bring their mixed blessings of conquest and manifest destiny. This time, it would be the Swedes.

According to a 12th-century chronicle, some 50 years before Rollo settled in Normandy, warring Slavic tribes 100 miles southeast of modern-day St. Petersburg entreated the Viking chieftain Rurik and his brothers Sineus and Truvor to rule over them and bring order. The brothers agreed and established three principalities.

Sometime after 862, Sineus and Truvor died, leaving Rurik to dominate the region from his royal fort above the river Volkhov. Known as Novgorod, or New Town, the land surrounding Rurik's fort grew into a key redoubt of the so-called Rus—possibly a corruption of the name for the people of Rodr, later known as Roslagen, the upland coastal region of eastern Sweden. From Rurik through Ivan the Terrible's son Fyodor, these Scandinavians reigned over what became Europe's largest medieval state—Russia.

Approximately a mile from modern Novgorod on a low hill overlooking the Volkhov's east bank, archaeologists have discovered a ninth-century fortification. The badly eroded site has recently yielded up a trove of Viking finds; among them, a silver pendant depicting a Valkyrie in flowing robes, an iron neck ring, and two bronze amulets with magical runic inscriptions averring, "You shall not be bereft of male strength!"

Skirted on three sides by the Volkhov and its tributaries, the settlement became an island during annual spring floods. The Arab geographer Ibn Rustah, writing in the early 10th century, described what may have been the nascent Novgorod: "Concerning the Rus, they live on an island which lies in a lake. [It] is three days journey in extent, and covered with woods and thick scrub. It is very unhealthy, and so marshy that the ground quivers when one treads on it." He went on to characterize the inhabitants: "They fight with the Slavs and use ships to attack them. They have no villages, no estates or fields. When a son is born the father will go up to the newborn baby, sword in hand; throwing it down, he says, 'I shall not leave you any property: you have only what you can provide with this weapon!' Their only occupation is trading in sable and squirrel and other kinds of skins, which they sell to those who will buy from them."

Novgorod lay athwart two lucrative Viking trade routes. Merchants from Sweden and the nearby island of Gotland made their way east across the Baltic and upriver to Novgorod, bringing cargos of pelts, beeswax, amber, and sometimes slaves. There, heading east or south, they rowed in convoy down the Volga and Dnieper rivers to the fabulous markets of Bulgar—capital of the spirited Slavonic tribe that ruled the Middle Volga—and then on to Constantinople. The more than 85,000 Arabic and 500 Byzantine coins unearthed in Scandinavia during modern times provide some small measure of the vitality of this eastern trade.

Intriguingly, well over half this total has turned up on Gotland. The island's mid-Baltic location and shelving beaches made it a favorite stopping-off place for Viking merchants plying the Eastern trade corridor. Through barter with these itinerants, native Gotlanders amassed grand fortunes, which they buried under houses and in

A carved wooden idol from 10th-century Staraja Ladoga in today's Russia is portrayed as limbless yet is bearded and clad in helmet, belt, and skirt. The figure may represent one of the gods Vikings reportedly invoked for assistance in their trading expeditions.

fields, away from prying eyes. In time, the island became a veritable treasure chest, its hills packed with silver. Today, farmers continue to free hoards from Gotland's sandy soil. One find, unearthed in 1936 at Stora Velinge, held 2,673 Arabic coins and a silver armband. All together, the trove weighed nearly 18 pounds.

Most of this treasure found its way from Russia to Gotland after the first quarter of the ninth century, but Rus entrepreneurs had initiated the eastward expansion earlier. They staked out trading posts in Lapland and the southern and eastern Baltic, collecting regular tribute from the surrounding peoples—many of whom were also nabbed as slaves.

Archaeological digs have turned up traces of two such fledgling market towns: at Apuole on Lithuania's Barte River, and 25 miles to the northwest in Latvia at Grobin. At both sites, earthworks, ruined forts, and cemeteries attest to the presence of thriving garrison towns. Of Grobin's three cemeteries, two contain burial mounds in which the charred bones of soldiers were found intermingled with their weapons. From the style of interment, excavators believe the men probably came from central Sweden. The third cemetery, made up of flat cremation graves, holds the remains of Gotlanders, including many women, their burned brooches still intact. Apuole likewise has graves of both Gotlanders and local residents. Apparently, populous communities of Gotlanders in Grobin and Apuole once hawked their goods under the protection of Swedish warriors.

The Rus did not venture much beyond these communities in the eastern Baltic until the second half of the eighth century when Muslim merchants bearing purses of Arab silver began appearing on the Don and Volga rivers. For the Norse, who had no silver resources of their own, this proved the ultimate enticement.

A silver pendant shaped as a Valkyrie and a dragon-headed dress pin made of lead characterize Viking grave goods found in Gorodishche, an early settlement in Russia. Evidence of manufacturing activity suggests that many such items were not imported but were produced by inhabitants of Scandinavian origin.

Handsomely crafted from two pieces of leather and decorated with spirals, a Scandinavian-style woman's shoe dates from the earliest settlement of Staraja Ladoga, a town that served as a gateway to trade with the East.

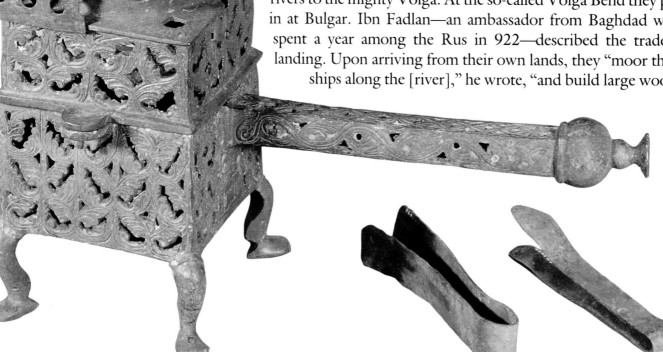

Designed to resemble a mosque, this bronze brazier with tongs surfaced in northern Sweden, thousands of miles from its Arabic point of origin. By virtue of their access to the waterways leading to the Arab world, Swedish Vikings controlled trade between Scandinavia and the East for many years.

Soon, Viking ship caravans were streaming eastward across the Gulf of Finland and moving up the Neva past the site where St. Petersburg would later rise to Lake Ladoga—the gateway to the markets.

Just seven miles south of the lake on the river Volkhov, excavators uncovered the remains of a late eighth-century town—nearly a quarter of a mile square and buttressed by earthen ramparts—that apparently served the Rus as a trading post and staging area. A bronze brooch, four bone gaming pieces, a bronze needle case, and shoes with stylish triangular heels—all of Swedish design—were unearthed amid the foundations of log houses. A stick incised with runic verse in the elaborate meter of ninth-century Scandinavian bards has led archaeologists to surmise that the Rus merchants were literate sorts, given to reciting court poetry.

No doubt such a diversion helped them to pass the time, for Staraja Ladoga, as the town is now called, seems to have been largely a city of transients. The majority of the traders lodged in its timber dwellings just long enough to transfer trade goods from their seagoing ships to smaller vessels more suitable for inland waterways. Made by local artisans, these canoelike boats—the largest of which measured 20 feet long and 9 feet wide—drew very little water, enabling the Viking traders to navigate the tangle of rivers, swamps, and streams leading south and east to the great trade routes beyond.

Most traders headed east along the Sias and Mologa rivers to the mighty Volga. At the so-called Volga Bend they put in at Bulgar. Ibn Fadlan—an ambassador from Baghdad who spent a year among the Rus in 922—described the traders' landing. Upon arriving from their own lands, they "moor their ships along the [river]," he wrote, "and build large wood-

These gilded 10th-century Islamic coins and belt mounts converted into pendants make up a part of Sweden's famed Vårby hoard. Its inventory, including beads exhibiting Chinese influence, demonstrates the many far-flung Eastern trading contacts made on the Vikings' travels down Russia's Dnieper and Volga rivers.

en houses on its banks. In one such house 10 or 20 people (or more, or less) will gather. Each of them has a bench on which he sits, and beside him sits one of the lovely girls assigned to these merchants."

It was also customary for newly arrived traders to seek divine patronage for their business transactions. According to Ibn Fadlan, a trader would first approach a timber peristyle containing a wooden idol surrounded by several small statues. Prostrating himself before the figures, he would begin his incantation, " 'Oh my Lord, I have come from far off with so many slave girls and so many sable furs. Now I come to you with this offering.' " He then placed bread, meat, leeks, milk, and beer before the idol and continued, " 'I want you to send me a merchant who has [lots of coins], who will buy from me as I wish, and will not contradict what I say.' "

If all went well on the rest of the journey, the trader made sacrifices of sheep and cattle at the same shrine on his return, saying, " 'My Lord has covered my needs. Now it is my duty to repay him.' " With these words, he laid a portion of the slaughtered meat before the idol and figures and gave the rest to the poor. In 1958 diggers at Staraja Ladoga—a halfway stop between Novgorod and the Baltic—unearthed a tall wooden figure from the remains of a small timber structure. Before the idol—carved to resemble a warrior— stood a hearth bearing the scorched bones of animals, birds, and fish. Here, perhaps, merchants had made their supplications and offered up their thanks.

The length and duration of trading trips varied widely. From Bulgar, Norsemen seeking added adventure might have picked up the 5,000-mile-long Silk Road east to China. More commonly, they followed the Volga south through the steppes to the land of the Jewish Khazars. A tolerant and cultivated people of Turkic descent, the Khazars maintained a standing army between the Caucasus and the Volga. For a tithe on their goods, the Rus were permitted access to the bazaars, where they sold furs and sword blades and bought well-honed Khazar spears and other items for resale along the shores of

A gold caste mark and silver inlaid eyes embellish an already elegant cast-bronze statuette of Buddha seated on a lotus throne that turned up on the island of Helgö, near Stockholm. Made in northern India around the fifth century, the figure traveled more than 5,000 miles to become a Viking keepsake.

the Caspian. From there, a few game merchants hired camels and went on to exotic Baghdad.

An archaeological find on the tiny island of Helgö near Birka provides tangible proof of this Far Eastern trade. In 1950 a man digging near his summer cottage turned up an ancient-looking bronze dipper and pieces of a silver bowl. Follow-on excavations conducted by the Swedish archaeologist Wilhelm Holmqvist revealed postholes and house footings, as well as fragments of spouted beakers, thousands of shards of European glass, iron padlocks, and bronze objects adorned with gilt. The site had evidently once supported a small but vital Viking trade mart—perhaps as early as the third century. But most astounding of all was the discovery of a bronze Buddha dating from the fifth century. The figurine could have traveled from India to Baghdad and then north—changing hands untold times—finally to be bartered, perhaps, for Rus pelts and carried to its last resting place in the soil of a Swedish island.

Not all the Rus launched their boats east from Lake Ladoga toward the Volga. Some struck out southward to the Black Sea and the marvels of Constantinople, whose markets overflowed with opulent wares from East and West. Tales of its golden-domed cathedrals, lighted streets, and luxury shops filled with exquisite merchandise must have stirred a powerful wanderlust in the avaricious Norsemen.

Even so, only the most intrepid adventurers took the approximately 1,300-mile-long Black Sea route, which led south along the river Volkhov to Novgorod, then up the river Lovat until its dwindling waters disappeared altogether. It was here that the travelers confronted the first of many portages, pulling their craft—goods and all—onto a row of logs, which they moved from stern to bow as the boat rolled forward. By such dogged and strenuous effort the Norse merchants gained the headwaters of the Dnieper River, their

The pine forest cemetery of Gnezdovo, a 10th-century settlement on the Dnieper River, is the largest Viking-age burial complex in Europe. The inhabitants of the fortified town were of Baltic, Slav, and Scandinavian heritage, and the spectacular Gnezdovo silver hoard (left) reflects this cultural mix.

pathway from the forests of the north to the Black Sea coast.

As more Rus frequented the route, fortified towns grew up at Gnezdovo, Smolensk, and Kiev. Artifacts from the sprawling Rus settlement at Gnezdovo, 300 miles south of Novgorod, have allowed scholars to resurrect something of what went on in these Viking river towns. According to Russian archaeologist Daniel Avdusin, jewelers, blacksmiths, and carvers turned a brisk trade here, repairing equipment and restocking travelers' wares.

About 4,500 grave mounds dot the pine forest east of Gnezdovo. Of the 700 or so burials so far unearthed, Burial Mound 13—the boat-cremation grave of a Viking chieftain and a young woman—is especially evocative of the Rus's funerary practices. Ibn Fadlan, who witnessed such a funeral beside the Volga in 922, wrote, "They gather his wealth and divide it into three—one part for his family, one part to provide clothes for him, and a third part for *nabidh* [a fermented beverage], which they drink on the day that the slave woman is killed and burned with her master."

According to Ibn Fadlan, the slave came forward and volunteered to be his bride in death and thus be burned with her master: By joining him in the grave, she would not only ennoble herself but gain eternal freedom. Meanwhile, the mourners hoisted the chieftain's boat up onto a large pyre of wood. "They then brought a bier which was placed in the ship; they covered it with Byzantine brocaded tapestries and with cushions of Byzantine brocade." Atop this tented mattress they placed the richly adorned corpse of the chieftain. "Then," continued Ibn Fadlan, "they brought *nabidh*, fruit, and sweet-smelling herbs and laid these beside him. Next they took two horses which they caused to run until they were sweating, after which they cut them in pieces and threw their flesh into the ship."

The young woman was then led to the boat. Men bearing

shields and staves approached her and gave her a beaker of nabidh. She sang a song and drained the beaker, after which she took another. While she lingered mournfully over her second drink, the old woman charged with killing her appeared. "The men beat with their staves on the shields so that her shrieks should not be heard and the other girls should not be frightened," wrote the Arab. "They laid her by the side of her dead master, then two took her legs, two took her hands, and the old woman, who is called the Angel of Death, put a rope round her neck and gave it to two men to pull; then she came with a dagger with a broad blade and began to thrust it time and again between the girl's ribs, while the two men choked her with the rope so that she died."

Afterward, the ship was set ablaze. "Soon it was burning brightly—first the boat, then the tent and the man and the maiden and everything in the boat."

The trade route to Constantinople continued south from Gnezdovo, following the Dnieper to Kiev, the Viking enclave some 570 river miles from the Black Sea. Until 862, according to monastic annals, Kiev was a small Slavic community on the river's steep west bank. Sometime soon thereafter, two of Rurik's lieutenants, Askold and Dir, converted the strategic site into a Rus stronghold. Then in 882 Oleg—prince of Novgorod and successor of Rurik—killed Askold and Dir, and with an army of Rus, Finns, and Slavs, captured Kiev, proclaiming it "the mother of Russian cities."

Traders passing through the city had to time their arrival. In winter the Dnieper was choked with ice and remained impassable until spring floodwaters receded. The Byzantine emperor Constantine VII Porphyrogenitus described the Viking merchants' preparation for the final leg of their journey in a 10th-century manual on foreign policy: "In the month of April, when the ice of the Dnieper has melted, they come back to Kiev. [There] they destroy their old canoes and buy fresh ones from the Slavs, who have been hewing them out during the winter in their forests. In June, the expedition sets out for [Constantinople]. For a few days the merchant fleet assembles at Vytechev, a fortress of the Rus just below Kiev."

The foundations of Vytechev can still be seen. Excavated between 1956 and 1958 by Russian academician B. A. Rybakov, the

fortress was discovered 35 miles below Kiev on the crest of a 235-foot hill overlooking the Dnieper. Beside the fortification, Rybakov identified the footings of a tower. Inside were bits of charred wood and tar-filled buckets used to fuel a beacon to warn the Rus of impending raids. Indeed, the Russian name has an Old Norse root, *viti,* meaning signal fire. Known as Vitaholm to the Vikings, the fortress was commemorated on at least one rune-stone back in Norway. It read: "Engle raised this stone after Torald his son who found death in Vitaholm between Ustaholm and Gardar." What an untimely end was Torald's; he was within six weeks of Constantinople.

Those six weeks, however, were fraught with extreme peril. At Dnepropetrovsk, a succession of granite gorges squeezed the Dnieper's waters into seven raging cataracts. Constantine VII characterized each one of them in his manual. Of the most notorious, Constantine writes, "At the fourth great rapid, which in Rus is called Aifor [Ever Fierce], everyone brings his ship to land and those who are to stand watch disembark." Sentinels were needed since the area was home to the Petchenegs, a vicious tribe who frequently ambushed travelers during the portage. "The rest [of the crew] take their belongings out of the [boats] and lead the slaves, fettered in chains, across the land for six miles, until they are past the rapids. After that they transport their vessels, sometimes by hauling them, sometimes by carrying them on their shoulders, past the rapids."

Four days of hard rowing finally brought the traders to the mouth of the Dnieper River. Here, on the island of Berezanj, archaeologists discovered

A conical silver cap mount and four silver tassel ends graced the hood of a man buried in Birka with his shield and two horses. The style and workmanship of the ornaments suggest that he may have been a warrior from the Hungarian southern steppes.

the only known rune-stone in Russia, a monument raised and dedicated by a Norseman named Grani to his friend Karl. Out of the mouth of the Dnieper, the Viking boats followed the Dniester to the Danube estuary, where they were fitted with sails, masts, and rudders for the voyage across the Black Sea.

When at last the domes of Byzantium appeared on the horizon, the exultation of the traders must have been palpable. How the ships arrayed in the harbor, the towering walls, and marble palaces must have dazzled the travelers' eyes as they sailed into the Golden Horn. Such grandeur could not help but ignite the greed of the Vikings, turning their thoughts from trading to conquest. Miklagard—or Great City, as the Rus called Constantinople—offered plunder on a scale that was beyond the wildest imagining of even the most rapacious of the Norsemen.

And so it was that, on the morning of June 18, 860, a fleet of 200 Viking warrior ships that had come down the Dnieper from Kiev was spotted moving over a calm sea toward the Byzantine capital. The Norsemen timed their attack with characteristic cunning. There

GOING BERSERK: A VIKING BATTLE TECHNIQUE

Of the many hundreds of words and place names that entered the English language from Old Norse, the one with the most horrid ring is *berserk*. And with good reason. To ensure victory against their enemies at home and on raids abroad, Viking chieftains often found it necessary to employ a class of rabid warriors known as berserkers, or bear-shirts, so called apparently because of the animal skins they wore.

Devotees of Odin, god of warriors and the entranced, berserkers followed his bidding —forgoing even the most sacred of ties, those of family— and rushed headlong into battle, perhaps under the influence of self-hypnosis, hallucinogenic mushrooms, or other narcotic substances. Sagas describe them as shrieking and leaping, sometimes naked, and oblivious to pain and injury. A 13th-century historian wrote that they were as "frenzied as dogs or wolves; they bit their shields; they were as strong as bears or boars; they struck men down, but neither fire nor steel could mark them."

Undoubtedly, some of the legends surrounding the berserkers were exaggerations, but contemporary accounts and artistic depictions of them offer substantiation of their conduct. Reliable literary references suggest that while berserkers were indispensable in a fray and as bodyguards to chieftains, their unstable behavior made them a menace. Indeed, some sagas portray them as persistent bullies, who are finally vanquished by the ancient texts' heroes.

had been no advance warning; the emperor and his fleet of galleys were away fighting Arabs to the east.

Over the next 10 days, the raiders attacked the surroundings of Constantinople with a fury surpassing anything that had been seen in the West. A homily delivered by the patriarch Photius in the aftermath of the raid wrenchingly expresses the Byzantines' sense of bewilderment at the cruelties that had been visited upon them: "An obscure nation, a nation of no account, dwelling somewhere far from our country, barbarous, nomadic, armed with arrogance has suddenly, in the twinkling of an eye, like a wave of the sea, poured over our frontiers, and as a wild boar has devoured the inhabitants of the land like grass. Infants were torn away from breast and milk and their bodies were dashed against the rocks which became their graves. Their mothers were slaughtered and thrown upon the still convulsing bodies of their infants. The flow of rivers was turned into blood; the fountains and reservoirs could not be distinguished because they were level with corpses."

Before this scourge, the citizens of Constantinople were helpless. The city's cathedrals resounded with the cry of penitents reciting litanies through the night. Photius, in a desperate attempt to attract divine assistance, carried a holy relic, a cloak believed to have been worn by the Virgin Mary, around the city walls and dipped it into the Bosporus. Within hours, the annals record, the Rus invaders left. Though medieval minds were quick to perceive a miracle, historians put the raiders' abrupt exit down either to Viking superstition or dread of the emperor's armada, due back any moment from the east.

The Rus returned to assail Miklagard in 907, 941, and 944. Each time, they extracted treaty terms more favorable than the last. Rus merchants were granted unlimited access to Constantinople's rich markets and provided with free food, shelter, and baths during their stay. The emperor, for his part, asked only for the right to recruit Rus mercenaries into the imperial guard. It was perhaps one of these, in a moment of bored pique, who carved runes in the marble balustrade of Constantinople's most illustrious cathedral, Hagia Sophia. Though now worn, they still spell the name "Halfdan."

A colorful 11th-century Byzantine mosaic depicts a member of the Varangian Guard, a corps of Viking mercenaries in the service of the Byzantine emperor. Young men from all over Scandinavia flocked to Constantinople to join the elite group for the perquisites and honor.

By the close of the 10th century, the Rus held sway over a vast territory that stretched from Lake Ladoga south to the Bosporus, and east from the Carpathian Mountains to the Volga. Under Svyatoslav—a third-generation, direct descendant of Rurik and the first of Kiev's rulers to bear a Slavic name—the Rus at last subdued the formidable Khazars and so-called Black Bulgar tribes along the Volga and also attacked the White Bulgar south of the Danube.

Gloomy and savage, Svyatoslav reportedly shunned all comforts, sleeping in the open with a saddle for his pillow. He shaved his head, except for a single forelock, and wore two pearls and a ruby suspended from one ear. On the battlefield, it was said, he fought with the fury of Odin, roaring like a wild beast, and his men "howling in a strange, disagreeable fashion." As might be expected, Svyatoslav met a violent end; returning from an engagement on the Danube in 972, he was ambushed at the Dnieper cataracts and killed by the Petchenegs, who gilded his skull and used it as a drinking cup.

Lines of runic inscriptions cover the shoulder area of a marble lion that once stood guard over the Athenian port city of Piraeus. Brought to Venice as booty in 1687, the sculpture's graffiti, although now illegible, offers graphic proof of the Viking presence in the Mediterranean.

Svyatoslav's son Vladimir brought the Rus realm its first patina of respectability. In 988, to further relations with Byzantium, Vladimir adopted Orthodox Christianity, driving his subjects en masse into the Dnieper to be baptized. Kiev was soon crowded with black-cloaked Byzantines, who, along with their knowledge, brought considerable wealth. Ukranian archaeologists have discovered several underground chambers thought to have been used by the Vikings for hoarding trading supplies and foodstuffs.

Vladimir's conversion won him the hand of the Byzantine emperor's sister. As recompense, Vladimir dispatched 6,000 Rus warriors to Constantinople to serve in the emperor's forces. Together with freelance Viking soldiers of fortune, they became known as the Varangian Guard—probably from the Old Norse *var,* meaning pledge, since they were pledged men. In battle, they formed the vanguard; in the streets and palace courts of Miklagard, they defended the emperor's person. Wrote Anna Comnena, daughter of Byzantine emperor Alexius I Comnenus, "As for the Varangians, they regard loyalty to the emperors and the protection of their persons as a family tradition, a kind of sacred trust and inheritance handed down from generation to generation; this allegiance they preserve inviolate and will never brook the slightest hint of betrayal."

Runic letters scratched into a parapet beneath the soaring dome of the Hagia Sophia basilica in Istanbul (ancient Constantinople) spell out the Viking name "Halfdan." Known to the Scandinavians as Miklagard, "Great City," the fabulous, treasure-filled Byzantine city must have seemed a fitting end to their long and punishing journey.

A tour of duty in the Varangian Guard was counted a consummate honor; from Russia and faraway Scandinavia, young men flocked to its standard. A rune-stone found at Ed near Stockholm proudly boasts of feats in the faraway Aegean: "Ragnvald let the runes be cut. He was in Greece, he was leader of the host." Besides good pay, a stint with the Varangians attracted much adulation, as evidenced by the saga of guardsman Bolli Bollasson: "He had a gilded helmet on his head and a red shield at his side on which a knight was traced in gold. He carried a lance in his hand, as is the custom in foreign lands. Wherever they took lodgings for the night, the womenfolk paid no heed to anything but to gaze at Bolli and his companions and all their finery."

The most famous of the Scandinavian hopefuls who traveled south to seek their fortunes in the Varangian Guard was the Norwegian Harald Sigurdsson. At 15, Harald—a charismatic youth with flaxen hair and one eyebrow higher than the other—fled Norway after his half-brother the king was killed in 1030 by mutinous jarls. Severely wounded himself, Harald sought refuge at the court of his kinsman Yaroslav the Wise, son of Vladimir and prince of Kiev.

A ruler of extraordinary political sensibilities, Yaroslav had guided the Rus empire into its Golden Age. Under his tutelage, Kiev amassed great wealth, its coffers bursting with the rich returns of a thriving north-south trade. He resurrected his ancestral ties to the West by taking a Swedish princess, Ingegerd, to wife and plotted the marriages of his three beautiful—and literate—daughters into the royal houses of Europe: Anna became queen of France, and Anastasia, queen of Hungary. The youngest, Yelisaveta, won the heart of young Harald, who for three years had been wielding ax and sword in the ranks of Yaroslav's army. But Yaroslav, loathe to have his daughter marry a throneless royal, discouraged the match.

Lovelorn, Harald headed down the Dnieper for Constantinople and the fabled Varangian Guard. By 1038 or so his valorous exploits from Sicily to Asia Minor to Palestine had catapulted him to the rank of commander of the guard. The gallant Harald showed as great a flair for gathering booty as he did for conquest. During his years with the guard, Harald accrued a fortune so enormous that, it was said, "no one in the northern lands had seen its equal in the possession of any one man." In 1044 he carted his treasure back to Kiev and laid it at Yaroslav's feet. Persuaded at last of Harald's merit, Yaroslav bestowed Yelisaveta's hand upon the famed warrior—now grown almost seven feet tall—and packed the couple off to Norway.

In 1047 Harald regained the crown lost by his brother. Known ever after as Harald Hardraade, or the Ruthless, the new king of Norway turned upon his Norse brethren, sailing his longship the *Great Dragon* throughout Scandinavia on expeditions of plunder and destruction. Harald stopped at nothing in his lust for fame and for absolute power.

In time, Harald's hawkish attentions lit upon the British Isles. King Edward the Confessor's death in 1066 had left Earl Harold Godwinson clutching the keys to the kingdom. Across the sea in Rouen, William the Bastard—the great-great-great grandson of the Viking Rollo—contested Godwinson's right to the throne. Not surprisingly, so did Harald Hardraade, whose destiny had been forged in Russia and Byzantium and who now ruled Norway with a Rus wife. Thus it was that the two great Viking dynasties of West and East cast covetous eyes upon England and readied their longships for what was perhaps the greatest conquest of all.

AN ART OF FIERCE VITALITY

Although they had a reputation for being a rough, violent people addicted to plunder and slaughter, the Vikings nevertheless took immense pride and delight in a vivid but surprisingly delicate form of art they made peculiarly their own—the intricate ornamentation of a wide variety of weapons and tools and other articles used in everyday life. Viking artisans embellished anything and everything with designs of dazzling complexity, decorating the woodwork and weather vanes of the Norse's proud ships, their broadswords and axes, the harnesses of their horses, the brooches both men and women wore to fasten their long capes, the walls of their buildings, the memorial stones they erected, and of course the caskets they used for storing heavy gold and silver jewelry and other signs of a person's wealth and power.

Viking artists had become masters at carving wood and casting metal ornaments by the early 800s—at the time the first raiding parties of fierce seafaring bandits set sail in search of slaves and booty—and they continued to create astonishingly ornate works for more than three centuries, until the very end of the Viking age. These Norse artists stuck always to a nature-inspired repertoire—mostly animals, including lions, snakes, fantastic imaginary beasts, and stylized birds of prey. In this, they were continuing a tradition evident in the savagely taloned and long-beaked eagle seen in the pre-Viking gilt-bronze Swedish harness ornament reproduced above. The ways the artists portrayed and combined such creatures changed, however, as time went on, and historians have divided Viking art into various styles, usually named after places in Scandinavia where important objects from each era were found. These styles as they succeeded one another are shown on the following pages through examples of masterpieces of Viking art. Sometimes grotesque, even brutal, the works display a technical brilliance and radiate the boldness and self-confidence of the Norse themselves.

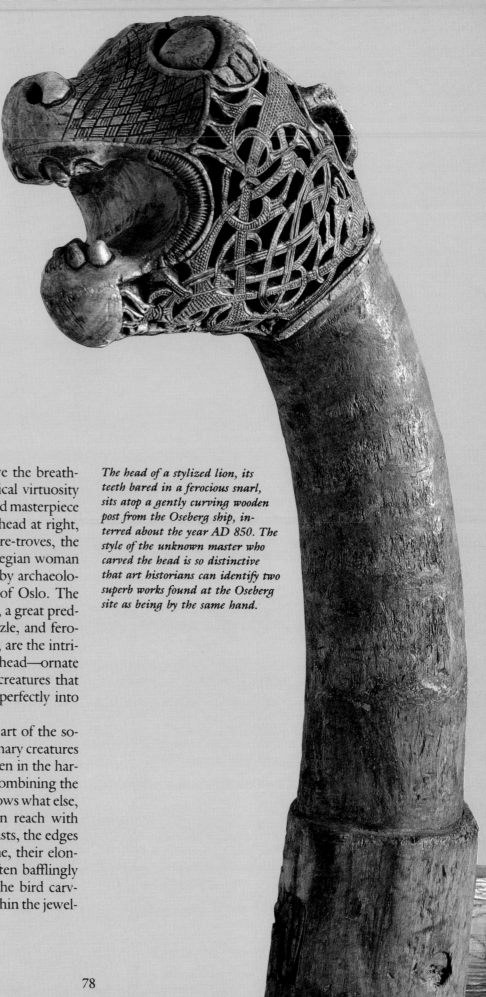

Even the earliest Viking works have the breathtaking barbaric energy and technical virtuosity that mark all Viking art. Undoubted masterpiece of this first era is the magnificent lion's head at right, found in the richest of all Viking treasure-troves, the ship used for the burial of a royal Norwegian woman that was unearthed nearly a century ago by archaeologists at Oseberg, not far from the city of Oslo. The Oseberg lion's face is astonishing in itself, a great predatory mask with staring eyes, blunt muzzle, and ferocious teeth. More amazing still, however, are the intricate carvings on the sides and top of the head—ornate and sinuous whirls of fantastic birdlike creatures that despite the complexity of the design fit perfectly into the lion's curving neck.

Adding a fierce vitality to other early art of the so-called Broa style is a race of strange imaginary creatures called "gripping beasts," which can be seen in the harness decorations on the opposite page. Combining the features of bears, lions, dogs, and who knows what else, these sinister figures grasp everything in reach with sharp claws—their own bodies, other beasts, the edges of the work of art itself. At the same time, their elongated bodies slither and intertwine in often bafflingly complex designs that nevertheless, like the bird carvings on the Oseberg lion, fit magically within the jewel-like objects they decorate.

The head of a stylized lion, its teeth bared in a ferocious snarl, sits atop a gently curving wooden post from the Oseberg ship, interred about the year AD 850. The style of the unknown master who carved the head is so distinctive that art historians can identify two superb works found at the Oseberg site as being by the same hand.

A sinuous, serpentlike beast makes an S-shape on top of a gilt-bronze harness decoration unearthed at the ancient town of Broa, on the island of Gotland, long a rich trading hub in the Baltic. Two other so-called gripping beasts with staring eyes seem to float on the sea at the bottom of the ornament.

Keeping a firm grip, a gnomelike creature stares from the top panel of another Broa-style harness mount. The other panels of the gilt-bronze casting teem with elongated animal forms that fill the oval recesses in the surface of the small but elaborate ornament.

Sometimes comic, sometimes menacing, gripping beasts continued to be a main feature in the two styles of Viking art that followed the Broa—the Borre and the Jellinge—which flourished almost simultaneously from the mid-800s into the second half of the following century. The strange gripping beasts were joined, though, by a new ribbonlike interlacing of bodies—which themselves often terminated in small animal heads that trailed long pigtails. The combination produced decorations of bewildering complexity—barbaric tangles that are virtually impossible for the eye to sort out but are also strangely beautiful, as in the rich, luminous Borre-style silver brooch at upper right. Even more impressive is the complex Jellinge-style giltbronze ornament for a wooden horse collar shown above. Ornately decorated animal heads cap each end, while the collar's ridge piece swarms with elegantly executed ribbon creatures with backward-turned heads. At top, the holes for the reins are arched with handsome geometric structures set off by two wonderfully lifelike predatory beasts. A marvel of expert casting, it remains a masterpiece of European metalwork.

Looking at first like a writhing mass of worms, the design of an exquisitely wrought brooch found in Denmark is actually a balanced composition. The ribbonlike bodies of beasts flow from four animal heads, each with a silver granule for an eye, that lurk near the center of the ornament.

Encrusted with a variety of animal shapes, including Jellinge-style ribbon creatures, a superb horse-collar ornament found at Sollested on the Danish island of Fyn rests on a substitute wooden support that replaced the long-since-rotted original. The name Jelling comes from a rich archaeological site on the Jutland Peninsula that was a 10th-century burial ground of Danish kings.

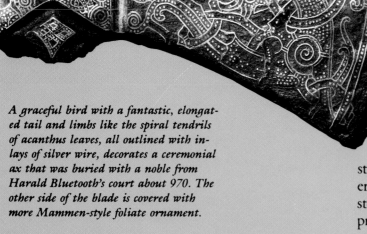

A graceful bird with a fantastic, elongated tail and limbs like the spiral tendrils of acanthus leaves, all outlined with inlays of silver wire, decorates a ceremonial ax that was buried with a noble from Harald Bluetooth's court about 970. The other side of the blade is covered with more Mammen-style foliate ornament.

Fascinated as always by animal forms, the Viking artists of the late 10th century began portraying new sorts of beasts, larger, fiercer, and even more vigorous than before. They began experimenting, too, with plant motifs, using them with a fresh, bold originality. The masterpiece of this new style—called Mammen after a site on Jutland where the ax blade above was found—is the massive stone erected at Jelling about the year 980 by the powerful Danish king Harald Bluetooth. Two faces of the stone display runic characters boasting of Harald's prowess and a stylized carving of the crucifixion, honoring the king's conversion to Christianity. But the third face of the great eight-foot-tall pyramidal stone bears the astonishing carving shown at right—a magnificent rampant lion with a huge snake entwined about its body, both animals radiating power and forming together one of the most impressive monuments in all Viking art. Almost as impressive in its own way is another triumph of Mammen art, the gleaming casket reproduced below, made of 22 sheets of elk horn bound with gilt-bronze bands, all the surfaces engraved with birds and animals caught up in twining convolutions of tendrils and leaves.

Sharp-beaked bird and animal heads emerge from the gilt-bronze bands that hold ornately carved sheets of elk horn to the wooden sides and top of an exact copy of the famous Cammin casket. Named for the Polish town of Cammin, whose cathedral owned it for centuries, the original casket vanished during World War II.

Standing out vividly from the Jelling stone's red-veined granite, King Harald Bluetooth's great carved lion with its strong legs and clawlike feet conveys an impression of power despite its elegantly small head and pointed ears. The tail, also in the new Mammen style, ends in a large acanthus leaf.

The last two periods of Viking art in many ways summed up the motifs—and the marvels—that had gone before. A lion and snake reminiscent of those carved on the Jelling stone dominate the ship's weather vane below, one of the finest examples of the Ringerike style of the late 10th and early 11th centuries, so called for the sandstone beds near Oslo where several ornamented stones have been found. In the Urnes period, named for the carved panels from an 11th-century wooden church at Urnes in Norway, the leafy plant motifs of the Mammen style turn into thickets of twining stalks and tendrils. Still, sup-ple, slithery animals also appear, some almost throwbacks to the gripping beasts. The elegant combination of plants and convoluted animal shapes in the panels from a doorway of the Urnes church *(right)* is a culmination of Viking artistry, a last glorious moment before Christian influences and the tide of Romanesque art, flooding into Scandinavia from Europe and England, put an end to purely Viking expression. By then the Vikings, their conquests of Normandy and England behind them, had ceased to be ferocious sea rovers and had largely been subsumed—the people, their culture, their art—in the great flow of European history.

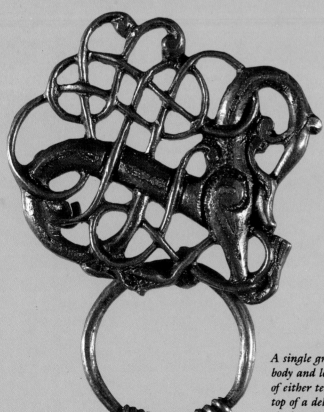

Enmeshed in the coils of a snake as well as tendrils, a lion, its head at right, its feet at left ending in a fleur-de-lis, dominates the design on a gilt-bronze weather vane that once swung from the prow of a longship. The vane is topped by a mythological beast that seems to scan the horizon.

A single graceful animal, its sinuous body and long tail enveloped by a swirl of either tendrils or a serpent, forms the top of a delicate openwork silver brooch in the late Urnes style found in Denmark.

A final triumph of Viking art, the outer panels of a portal of Norway's 11th-century Urnes church combine four-legged animals that are as slim as greyhounds and serpentine creatures that bite each other's necks and form large, looping, figure-eight patterns.

A VIKING STAMP ON THE BRITISH ISLES

This Celtic figure, one of two enameled fittings that secured a handle to an eighth-century Irish or Scottish bucket, likely caught the eye of a Viking raider. Archaeologists found the pail on the Oseberg ship in 1904.

Engrossed in prayers or at their labors, cultivating a garden of healing herbs, brewing mead, or applying the final brush strokes of luminous color to a newly copied Gospel, the monks of the English abbey on Lindisfarne, a tiny island off the North Sea coast of England, probably never imagined themselves as lambs about to be slaughtered. But at some dark hour of the eighth day of June in the year 793, a band of fair-haired Norsemen lowered the masts of their high-prowed longships, and as silent and sudden as the haar—the cold, thick fog that often cloaks such coastlines—they slipped ashore, intent on mayhem.

According to Simeon of Durham, a 12th-century chronicler with access to a long-lost northern version of the *Anglo-Saxon Chronicle,* the raiders descended upon the community like a pack of wolves or a swarm of stinging hornets. With blades and bloodcurdling yells, they ripped through chapels and dormitories, barns and workshops, killing and maiming some of the innocents and carrying off others to sell as slaves. The Vikings pried the jewels from reliquaries and shrines, tore the elaborately wrought gold and silver casings from the holy books, ransacked and burned, then whirled off to sea again, bearing their prisoners and plunder.

Shocked and battered survivors spread their story throughout the royal courts and religious houses of Christian Europe. The scholar Alcuin, in attendance upon the Holy Roman Emperor Charlemagne at his court in Aachen, wrote to the highest churchmen of England and the king of Northumbria, of which Lindisfarne was part, to express his horror. "Never before," he declared, "has such a terror appeared in Britain, and never was such a landing from the sea thought possible." The catastrophe, he opined, was an act of divine chastisement against members of religious orders who had slackened in their zeal and a warning to all who had lapsed in their faith.

Other observers recalled that the early months of the year had been fraught with terrible omens—fiery dragons in the sky, giant whirlwinds, and bolts of lightning, followed by a great famine. And the grim events would prove to be only a foretaste of more raids to follow, as the Vikings returned the next year, not to Lindisfarne but to a monastery some 50 miles to the south that Simeon of Durham identified as Jarrow. Severe storms wrecked many of the raiders' ships and allowed the local population to get its own back by slaughtering those Norsemen who struggled ashore. But the defeat did not deter the raiders from hitting island and coastal monastic communities throughout the British Isles in the decades to come. Irish annals, for instance, describe "devastation of all the islands of Britain by the gentiles" in the year 794 and speak of "great devastation between Ireland and Scotland" in 798. Only bad oceangoing weather, it seemed, offered relief. One Irish monk, hard at work copying a sacred text, could scarcely contain his joy at the sounds of a storm boiling up outside the scriptorium window. In the margin of his manuscript, he wrote, "There's a wicked wind tonight, wild upheaval in the sea; no fear now that the Viking hordes will terrify me."

The seaborne raiders the monk dreaded were not a random disaster, sent like a plague of boils or a bad harvest to add to their victims' trials and sorrows; they were the advance guard of a great westward move-

Thought to be Vikings, these warriors, as depicted by Anglo-Saxons, brandish swords and axes on a 10th-century memorial stone from the site of Lindisfarne (far right). *The raiders laid waste to the priory in 793, heralding the dawn of the Viking age in the British Isles.*

ment of aggressive and resourceful Scandinavian settlers. Nor were they a uniform group. Some hailed from Norway's harsh, rocky coast and were drawn to those northern and western parts of the British Isles with landscapes similar to the fjords and hills of home. Others sailed from Denmark and looked covetously upon areas of England reminiscent of the low-lying, fertile farmlands they had left.

Over the course of the ninth century, the Norse seized control of parts of Ireland, the Orkney and Shetland islands in the north, the Hebrides in the west, the Isle of Man in the Irish Sea, and much of England. They overpowered native chieftains, established colonies, farmed the land, built trading settlements that grew into cities, and warred among themselves. In Ireland and England they even reigned as kings. No doubt the invaders were changed by those they conquered: They eventually intermarried with the local population and abandoned their pantheon of pagan gods in favor of Christianity. Yet the Vikings would dominate some of the islands until the late 11th century, when a new wave of conquerors, the Normans who were themselves of Nordic descent, swept them away.

The physical signs of the Viking presence would remain for modern archaeologists to find, in the form of graves and grave goods, farmsteads, settlements, workshops full of tools, even carefully buried hoards of coins, jewels, fine ornaments, and additional treasures. Yet the Vikings also left traces of another kind, less tangible than grave goods but not as vulnerable to the ravages of time—a rich collection of Nordic placenames, personal names, words, and accents. Relics of the Viking presence, they carry clues to the lives and movements of the settlers and to their relationships with their world.

So too do the accounts of those who lived at the time, witnesses to or players in its dramas—the Celts of Ireland and western Scotland, the Britons in the southwestern Scottish kingdom of Strathclyde, the Picts of the east and north, the Angles and Saxons of the English kingdoms. Their voices today are faint but persistent. Some come embellished beyond the limits of strict reportage by generations of early medieval chroniclers or through the filter of folk memory—embedded in tales, songs, and local traditions. Yet these breathe life into the silent fragments uncovered by archaeologists.

The raiding season opened in the spring, when prevailing easterly winds helped speed the longships across the North Sea. After establishing base camps on small, easily defended islands off the Scot-

The Howardian Hills area in Yorkshire, plotted at right, offers valuable clues to Viking settlement patterns. Fryton, for instance—an English village probably taken over and renamed by a Dane—shares arable land north of the hills with Hovingham, Barton-le-Street, and other English villages and farms, while the Viking-named villages of Brandsby, Stearsby, Skewsby, and Dalby sit on less desirable, previously unoccupied land to the south. Also identified as Viking in origin by the "thorpe" in their names, Wiganthorpe, Howthorpe, and the other thorpes date to a later phase of Scandinavian colonization. As shown above, parishes with Scandinavian names (dots) ultimately blanketed northern and eastern England, that is, Northumbria and the Danelaw, a region under Danish control and legal organization.

tish and Irish coasts or along the shores of sheltered bays and estuaries as other Vikings were doing along the northern edge of continental Europe, the Norsemen spent the summer plundering. Then, when the autumn winds rose up from the southwest, the Vikings loaded their ships with booty and set sail for home to wait out the winter.

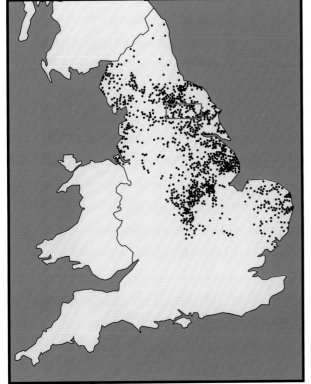

Of the Norsemen's initial raids and early clashes with the natives, little hard archaeological evidence remains apart from the remnants of some earthworks that may have been built for defensive purposes on headlands in the northern isles. Even on the repeatedly raided Iona, one of the smallest of the Inner Hebrides islands west of mainland Scotland, where excavations of ancient buildings have turned up signs of burning, researchers hesitate to claim that the ashes record anything other than home-grown catastrophes caused by a stray ember from a hearth or an insufficiently snuffed-out candle.

The Norsemen did not attack Iona and its sister monasteries out of any crusading zeal against Christian monotheism but because these sites—with their rich stores of sacred objects decorated with jewels and precious metals, their fat livestock, and well-filled granaries—offered the richest pickings. The Vikings learned the calendar of Christian festivals and timed their visits to coincide with these dates. That way, the intruders could count on abundant food, a large harvest of brooches, belt

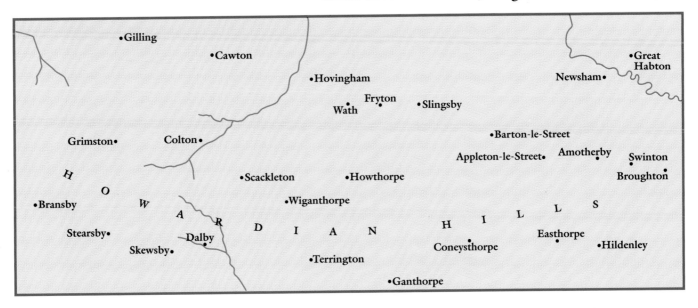

XP AVTEM

GENERA

SI ERAT EVM ESSE IDS

PONSATA MATER EIVS

MARIA IOSE DANTE CVM

CONVENIRENT INVENTA

EST IN VTERO HABENS

buckles, and any other goods that they coveted—and slaves.

The Vikings made considerable use of such human booty. Norse texts report, without need for comment, on the buying and selling of at least one Irish princess who "served faithfully" in the household of a Norse earl's wife. But even greater profit was derived from the export of Scottish and Irish captives, apparently much in demand in the slave markets of the Mediterranean.

Sometimes, in time-honored piratical fashion, the Vikings demanded protection money from their unwilling hosts. The *Annals of Ulster,* for instance, relate that in 798 the pagans took "tribute from the provinces" but nevertheless went on to vandalize the shrine of Dochonna, a local saint.

For a lucrative sideline, particularly valuable prizes could be held to ransom. A magnificent illuminated manuscript of the four Gospels, made by English scribes in Canterbury, bears a note in its margins—written in ninth-century Anglo-Saxon script—announcing that "I, Earl Alfred, and Werberg, my wife, have acquired this book from a heathen army with our true money, that is, with pure gold, and this we have done for the love of God and for the good of our souls, and because we are not willing that this holy book should remain any longer in heathen hands."

Back in the Nordic homelands, modern archaeology bears witness to the success of the marauders. Almost half of the artifacts of Irish origin dating from the Viking era have been found not in Ireland but on Scandinavian soil. Historians debate whether this glittering treasure trove—gilt-bronze statuettes of saints, elaborate metal mounts ripped from sacred books, intricately carved crosiers, and handsome bronze brooches—arrived there as plunder or as the fruits of peaceable trading. But at least one reliquary, its surfaces lovingly adorned with a design of interlaced ribbons, bears the roughly carved announcement on its base that it is now the sole property of a Norse woman named Rainvaig—perhaps a raider's gift home to his wife or his daughter.

As the ninth century drew on, the visitors showed less inclination for the trek home. Norwegians may have established some sort of pirate settlements on the Shetland and Orkney islands by the time of the raids on Lindisfarne, and by 841 Vikings in Ireland were operating out of fortified bases located at Dublin and Annagassan, about 40 miles to the north. In the Hebrides, the Norse presence was so well established by the middle of the ninth century that the

Old English notes are penned above and below the Latin text of Saint Matthew's Gospel (left), part of an illuminated manuscript from Canterbury, now in Stockholm, known as the Codex Aureus. The notes recount how an earl and his wife ransomed the book from a "heathen army"—Vikings—in the ninth century.

This highly decorative ninth-century gilt-bronze Northumbrian book mount was apparently Viking loot from a raid on an English monastery. The piece turned up in Norway, where it had been converted into a woman's pendant.

chain became known as the Isles of the Foreigners. Farther south and east, Danish Vikings set their sights on England, where sporadic raids soon gave way to outright invasion by well-disciplined armies. In 851 one English chronicler reported, with heavy heart, that for the first time "the heathen stayed through the winter." The Norsemen would menace his countrymen for generations to come. In 865 an army estimated to have numbered between 500 and 2,000 men disembarked in East Anglia, the easternmost English kingdom, and easily pierced the coastal defenses. Supplied with horses by the inhabitants, who had seen the wisdom in quickly coming to terms of peace, the invaders then traced the footsteps of another foreign force, the Romans, who had preceded them to the island nine centuries earlier. Intent on speeding overland travel, the Romans laid out thousands of miles of roads reaching from Canterbury in the southeast to Exeter in the southwest and as far north as York, at the confluence of the Ouse and Foss rivers. These thoroughfares survived in sufficiently good condition to do the same favor for the Vikings, who later toured the roads on mounts brought from home.

Hoards of coins dating from the periods of invasion testify to the terror subjects of the kingdoms of East Anglia, Mercia, and Northumbria likely felt when they learned of the approaching foreign army. Throughout the 800s, the authors of the *Anglo-Saxon Chronicle* described English and foreign armies meeting in battle, great slaughters on both sides, and forced migrations. Panicked by news of such hardship, many residents must have buried their valuables for safekeeping and then fled, never to return, leaving for modern archaeologists a record of Danish progress through the land.

By 880 only the southwestern kingdom of Wessex remained free of Viking domination, largely because of its enterprising ruler, Alfred the Great. Hoping to minimize Viking plunder, Alfred ordered construction of a chain of forts, as well as town fortifications, so that the peasantry would be protected when the Danes appeared. Then, to defend the coast, he had a fleet of new warships built—

heavy vessels of the king's own design, with tall sides and shallow drafts, which made them hazardous for the enemy to board and maneuverable even at low tide.

Alfred's greatest accomplishment, however, was not military but diplomatic. Hoping to signal his intention to live in peace with his new neighbors, he signed a treaty with the Danish leader Guthrum in 886, in which Alfred acknowledged Viking conquest of the territories lying north and east of Wessex. The accord had a calming influence on the Vikings, who subsequently regarded the area not as alien territory but as home. Totaling some 25,000 square miles and bounded in the south by a line running northwest from London to Chester on the Irish Sea and in the north by a line running from the mouth of the river Tees to the North Channel of the Irish Sea, this region would come to be known as the Danelaw.

The Scandinavians imported many things to the area—their language, their culture, and as the name implies, their own long-standing legal customs. A law code written in the Danelaw in the last years of the 10th century, for instance, declares that courts should be made up of 12 men of substance from the community who should vow impartiality toward those brought for trial and vote to reach a verdict. "If they differ," the law reads, "let that stand which eight of them have pronounced."

The Norsemen would have a similar impact on Ireland. When the Vikings first arrived there, they found a sparsely settled, entirely rural land. Its large, well-organized monastic communities housed scholars, artisans, and scribes whose attainments were the envy of Christian Europe, yet its economy was primitive and its lay population poor. The Roman Empire's rule had never reached this island on the western edge of the European world; the legacy of legal and administrative

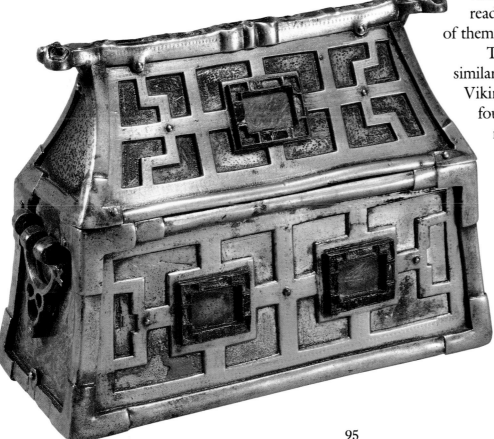

Runes on the base of this eighth- or ninth-century reliquary declare, "Rainvaig owns this casket." Possibly carried away by a pagan raider, whose wife, Rainvaig, claimed the box, it was later used again in a church for religious purposes. The box still contains relics.

structures that formed a common bond between the inhabitants of other parts of Europe was absent.

Politically, Ireland consisted of a precarious patchwork of petty kingships that were ruled by mutually mistrustful chieftains. Too absorbed in their own rivalries, they failed to unite against the invaders. In fact, according to contemporary accounts, in a period that saw 26 attacks by Vikings, Irish warlords raided each other's territory 87 times. None of the combatants, apparently, heeded the cries of one of their own chroniclers: "Alas, it is pitiful for the Irish to continue the evil habit of fighting among themselves, and that they do not rise together against the Norwegians."

Technological inferiority only compounded the natives' problems, making it easy for the Norsemen to move in and take over. Irish boats, for example, were no more than the skin-

Preservationists converge on Dublin's Christ Church Cathedral on September 23, 1978, to decry planned construction on a Viking site at adjacent Wood Quay. An estimated 17,800 protesters took part. When bulldozers threatened to resume demolition in 1979, activists made headlines by occupying the site. Among the campers was city council member Sean Dublin Bay Rockall Loftus, seen at right telling a worker to lay down his tools.

covered wickerwork vessels, or coracles, that the fishermen had used for thousands of years. Moreover, Irish clubs and axes splintered under the assault of Viking broad, sturdy slashing swords, axes, and spears with blades more than a foot and a half long.

At least in one instance, however, guile proved able to outdo armaments. Irish chronicles recount how a Norwegian prince by the name of Thorgils led an invasion force of 10,000 men against the greatest of Ireland's holy houses—the monastery at Armagh, some 35 miles to the southwest of present-day Belfast. After harrying the abbot off the premises, Thorgils announced that he would take over as high priest and make the place a temple to pagan gods. Then, to affirm his control over the territory, he erected a chain of defensive earthworks from Armagh to the kingdom of Connaught more than 100 miles to the west.

Legend has it that the daughter of Maelsechlainn, ruler of Meath in east-central Ireland, later invited Thorgils and 15 of his bravest captains to join her and a bevy of maidens for a romantic rendezvous on the shore of Lough Owel, a small lake in modern Westmeath County. When the Norsemen arrived, it is said, the princess's companions slipped out of their gowns and revealed themselves to be a band of hairy male warriors, who wrestled the Vikings into the water and drowned them.

The episode, if true, had little effect on the rapacious Vikings. On the shores of several estuaries, they built wooden forts to serve as winter shelters and as bases for their raids around the Irish coast. Within a few decades, these bolt-holes acquired a more permanent character, expanded in size, and evolved into a type of settlement that, according to all available archaeological evidence, was completely new to Ireland—towns.

Nearly a thousand years later, in the 1850s, laborers building new sewers and roadways for the city of Dublin would uncover dramatic proof of these developments. Digging into what they thought was only boggy soil, they brought to light the decayed debris of a millennium of continuous habitation: bronze pins, bone combs, horseshoes, and other articles. Local antiquarians identified the finds as concrete evidence of Dublin's Viking past.

In 1866 railway workers at Kilmainham, a suburb on the river Liffey just west of the city's center, unearthed a large ninth-century cemetery that contained the graves of Viking men and women. The men had been interred with their swords and spears laid alongside them, the women with oval brooches that somewhat resemble tortoiseshells, an ornament found in women's burials throughout the Viking world. The presence of both sexes made it clear that this was a resting place not only for fallen raiders but also for Norse families who made their homes in Ireland.

When archaeologists in the late 1960s and in the 1970s dug into the soil of Wood Quay, a 4½-acre riverfront site in central Dublin, they found even more evidence of the Scandinavian presence: an early 11th-century fortified town built upon a 10th-century permanent settlement. The discovery was of extraordinary historical importance, yet the site failed to capture wide public interest until November 1977, when it was learned that construction workers were

FACE TO FACE WITH EYMUND THE FISHERMAN

A knife in one hand and a fish in the other, the dramatic wax and foam mannequin known as Eymund the Fisherman (far right) sits atop a barrel in a re-created Jorvik street scene in a York museum, gazing out at passersby much as he might

have done over 1,000 years ago.

Eymund is the product of a remarkable new computer-assisted technique, designed for scanning and measuring patients undergoing facial surgery

at London's University College Hospital. Working from the remains of Viking skeletons found in 1986 at York, scientists hoped to reconstruct ancient faces through historical detective work and the latest advances of forensic science.

Cracks and fissures repaired with plaster of Paris, a Viking skull revolves on a turntable as a laser sweeps over its surface, feeding data into a computer image bank.

Next, a living volunteer receives a dusting of talcum powder, a reflective substance that helps the computer read contours of his hair.

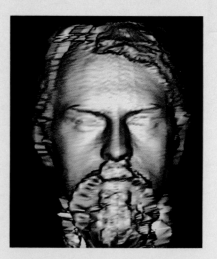

With the results of both scans converted into three-dimensional images, the computer superimposes the living face over the Viking skull, creating a model for the sculpture.

about to bulldoze a thousand-year-old Viking wall so that a municipal office complex could be erected.

Almost overnight Wood Quay became the focal point for a bitter dispute between architects and developers on one side and archaeologists and preservationists on the other. Angry that a place the Irish people valued was about to be assaulted once again by blade and by hammer, protesters took to the streets, carrying models of Viking shields, banners bearing slogans, and posters crying, "Save Viking Dublin!" and "God Save Our Vikings!"

After political and legal battles lasting three years and involving archaeologists, the High Court, the city government, and the general public, construction was finally allowed to proceed—but not

After being repaired and patched with plaster of Paris, the skull of a 30-year-old male was scanned carefully by a low-power laser beam that fed the contours and dimensions into a powerful computer, producing a three-dimensional electronic image. Next, a human volunteer —of size and build similar to the Viking subject—underwent a similar laser scan. The computer then adapted the modern face to the shape of the ancient skull, effectively stretching the living skin over the dead bone like a rubber mask. With this hybrid image serving as a template, a computer-controlled milling machine sculpted a three-dimensional bust from a block of polyurethane foam.

Finally, a sculptor set to work animating the face, her artistic skill fueled by an understanding of the era. Knowing, for instance, that many Vikings suffered from intestinal parasites, she gave the figure's skin a sallow color.

In his final form, Eymund makes a striking impression, one that might startle his own family. With his piercing eyes and hauntingly lifelike expression, the figure comes close to allowing modern observers a glimpse of the true face of the past.

An artist adds the finishing touches of hair, eyes, and skin color and the reconstruction comes vividly to life as Eymund the Fisherman (right).

before a program of careful excavations revealed the foundations of rectangular houses set in individual plots of ground bounded with pathways and facing onto clearly delineated streets.

Within the remains of these buildings, the excavators uncovered hundreds of thousands of artifacts, proving the existence of a busy community of traders and artisans. Scraps of bone, deer antlers, slender pins, and nails indicate that comb makers, bronzesmiths, and coopers plied their trades there. Woodturners manufactured items such as spindles, handles, and gaming boards and the pieces that would be played upon them. Shoemakers and other leatherworkers fashioned pouches and assorted goods while casting away great quantities of scrap material. And a weaver—probably one of many—worked weft and warp threads together with a small wooden tool lovingly carved into the shape of a sword.

The Norse stamp on this material was unmistakable. A brooch of gilt bronze bears decorations identical to those on many 10th-century brooches found in Scandinavia. A soapstone mold holds a matrix for casting Thor's hammers, the tiny good-luck amulets favored by Vikings of the day. Iron spearheads, beads of jet and glass and amber, remnants of weighing scales used by traders—all bear the marks of Norse influence.

Archaeologists also found evidence that Dublin had become an increasingly active port by the late 10th century. Excavations revealed embankments to protect the town from the incursions of the river Liffey, as well as the remnants of quays and ships' masts, an early breakwater, and other signs of a busy waterfront. Even more significant were the many artifacts of foreign origin—glazed pots from England, a German garnet, walrus ivory from the Arctic, Baltic amber, silk from the Levant, pieces of purplish red porphyry possibly from Rome, Saxon ivories, and medicinal drugs from France—all dating from the 10th and 11th centuries.

Yet Dublin—most important of several Viking-built trading towns, including Limerick, Wexford, Cork, and Waterford—was not necessarily the final destination for foreign goods. Hoards of 9th- and 10th-century silver, most of it imported, have been found throughout the Irish countryside. Much of the precious metal, scholars say, likely passed through Dublin. Such distribution shows how radically the Vikings transformed the economic life of Ireland. Before their arrival, such commerce as existed was based on barter, and the exchange of goods took place mainly within the orbit

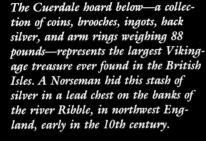

of the monasteries. The Norse created towns as centers for trade and introduced the notion of hard currency. Only with the newcomers did the Gaelic language acquire words, borrowed from the Norse vocabulary, for such new concepts as "market" and "penny."

At some point in the last decade of the 10th century, the Dubliners set up their first mint and began production of coins modeled on prototypes turned out in such English towns as Norwich, Chester, London, and Exeter. Archaeologists came across the English currency in sizable quantities while digging at Wood Quay. Evidently, say the experts, long before the establishment of the local mint, trade across the Irish Sea was so vigorous that the Dubliners hoarded the coins for use in English ports.

The Norse presence was equally strong in Scotland and on the Isle of Man, located in the Irish Sea, roughly midway between Ireland and England. Surviving placenames in these regions attest to the spread of Norse settlement. Of the 126 village names on the Isle of Lewis, one of the Outer Hebrides, for instance, 110 either are totally Scandinavian or have some Norse element within them.

No written texts describe these settlers' activities firsthand. Three hundred years of silence lie between the accounts of early raids penned by ninth-century Irish chroniclers and the narratives compiled by Icelandic saga writers in the late 1100s. For archaeologists, however, a wealth of material fills the gap—pagan and Christian graves, the excavated remains of rural settlements, and silver hoards.

Apparently, anxious natives were not the only ones to bury their valuables in Scotland and on the Isle of Man. The Vikings themselves commonly stored such goods underground for safekeeping, digging them up only when the owner wanted something or when the time had come to move on. The hoards are conspicuous by the presence of coins from many different countries, by jewelry crafted in distinctively Norse design, and by silver arm and neck rings. Since the metal was used as a form of payment, these rings were frequently produced in standard weights and could be cut into pieces corresponding to coin weights. Coins themselves were sometimes clipped into halves and quarters. Known as hack silver, this improvised currency was used in Scotland by Viking settlers, as it was by Norse in other parts of Europe. Of 40 Scottish hoards known to

archaeologists, 31 bear the clear marks of Scandinavian ownership.

A few caches have turned up in places outside the areas of Norse settlement, indicating the movements of Vikings engaged in specific military campaigns. Dated coins in a hoard from Kirkcudbrightshire in southern Scotland, for instance, suggest that the person who buried them may have been a follower of either Ivar the Boneless, the chieftain who captured the native fortress of Dumbarton Rock in 871, or Halfdan, who harried the Britons of Strathclyde as well as their Pictish neighbors to the northeast in 875.

For most Scandinavians in Scotland, however, day-to-day existence did not begin and end with the excitements of warfare and pillage. Excavations of such settlements as Jarlshof in the Shetland Islands and around Orkney's Bay of Birsay suggest that their patterns of life and work deviated little from those of their kinfolk back in the ancestral homelands. The settlers favored sites amenable to seafaring, fishing, and farming. These were generally near the shore, with easy access to a sheltered spot where a boat could be safely beached, and possessed enough level, well-drained ground to build a farmstead and plant crops. Farther inland lay tracts of grazing ground. In the Shetlands, where good upland soil was scarce, these were probably shared out among a community of neighboring farmers.

At both Birsay and the farm at Jarlshof, archaeologists found layers of occupation dating back to the Bronze Age. Analyzing the traces of bone material and plants unearthed at these sites, researchers concluded that the crops and the livestock of the Vikings differed little from those of their Pictish and earlier predecessors. Half of the bones found in the refuse heaps came from cattle, 30 percent from sheep, 20 percent from pigs. The principal grains in the local diet were oats and barley.

The Norse's houses were much like those at home. Some were of impressive size: The earliest Jarlshof building, dated to the ninth century, extends approximately 70 feet from end to end. Such structures could well have been the residences of the larger-than-life but apparently historic figures who populated the narratives of 13th-century Icelandic storytellers. According to the author of the *Orkneyinga Saga*, for instance, Svein Asleifarson, the swashbuckling proprietor of one of these northern farmsteads, spent his winters on the one-mile-long island of Gairsay, northeast of the island of Mainland, where, in the interest of creating a good name for himself, he entertained some 80 men at his own expense.

The 17th-century laird's house ruins at upper right of this aerial view of Jarlshof in Scotland stands roughly parallel with a Viking long house whose floor has been covered with white sand for heightened visibility. The ruins of later Viking structures that were built at right angles to the long house can be seen in the center of the photograph.

"His drinking hall," says the saga, "was so big there was nothing in Orkney to compare with it. In the spring he had more than enough to occupy him, with a great deal of seed to sow, which he saw to carefully himself. Then, when that job was done, he would go off plundering in the Hebrides and in Ireland on what he called his 'spring trip,' then back home just after midsummer, where he stayed till the cornfields had been reaped and the grain was safely in. After that he would go off raiding again till the first month of winter was ended. This he used to call his 'autumn trip.' "

Much of what is known about the daily lives of the earliest Viking settlers, however, has been gleaned not from such sagas but from graves. For a generation or two, the new arrivals followed the pagan burial practices of their homeland and interred their dead with the possessions that they had prized in life. The grave goods of a Norse woman from a settlement among the rich farmlands at Westness in Orkney, for instance, included a magnificent jeweled brooch of Celtic design, a pair of the traditional tortoise-type brooches worn by most Scandinavian women of the age, a string of 40 intricately decorated beads in variegated patterns and colors, a bone comb, and various small ornaments of carved bronze. Alongside lay the tools of her working life: a curved sickle blade and various small implements for making cloth, including a whalebone plaque that may have served to press down seams or soften leather, a set of shears, and other implements for weaving and—possibly—knitting textiles for her household's use.

Likewise, at Kiloran Bay on the Hebridean island of Colonsay—where Viking relics have been found at a place with a Gaelic name meaning Hillock of the Foreigners—archaeologists discovered a ninth-century Viking man buried in a boat probably his own. Its wooden frame had rotted away, but its rivets survived. With him were all the tools of a warrior's trade, including a sword, a round

A boat-shaped cairn marks the grave of a one-time Norse inhabitant of Balladoole on the Isle of Man. Archaeologists discovered the bones of a cremated horse, an ox, a pig, a sheep or goat, a dog, and a cat—possible gifts to the dead—in a sandy layer above the stones.

The remains of a Viking man lie with his weapons and a few tools in an 18-foot-long boat grave at Westness, Orkney. Archaeologists could approximate the contours of the wooden boat, which had long since deteriorated, by carefully recording the location of the iron rivets that once held it together.

shield, a battle-ax, a spear, several arrowheads, and a horse, still in its harness with bronze mounts, that had been slaughtered to accompany its master in the afterlife.

The grave also contained a set of impressive bronze scales, equipped with a balance beam and seven lead weights in various sizes, decorated with carved metalwork or enamel. Similar scales have been found in many Viking graves; their obvious purpose was to weigh out precious metals. Some scholars suggest that the Colonsay Viking was a merchant who took up arms to defend himself on his trading voyages; others speculate that he was a warrior chieftain who used the scales to give his men their fair and proper share of plundered silver. But whatever his occupation may have been, he—or those who buried him—had begun to mingle Christian beliefs with pagan tradition, for two of the stone slabs that surrounded his tomb bore large carved crosses.

On the Isle of Man, other burials mark a period of transition between the Vikings' old and new belief systems. In Balladoole, a Norse chieftain lies in a Christian cemetery, but his grave is pagan: Not only does he rest under a mound and in a ship, but he also has his weapons. One of his fellow warriors, interred in a churchyard at Ballateare, clung to enough of the old faith to require that a female slave be sacrificed—by a blow to the skull—at the time of his passing.

By the end of the 10th century, the conversion of the Vikings on Man seems to have been virtually completed. Few mounds above burials enclosing grave gifts have been found from this period. Instead, the Vikings—or at least those with the silver to do so—marked the resting places of their dead with lavishly carved slate crosses. Though their shapes echoed the cross slabs of Ireland and Pictland, their decorations show a fusion of native and characteristically Scandinavian styles: interlaced serpents, fantastical winged creatures peering out of a jungle of twisted vines, scenes from Norse mythology, figures of warriors—pagan heroes, perhaps, or dragon-slaying saints—clasping spears or mounted on horseback.

One of their makers, whose signed works survive on the Isle of Man, was a sculptor with the patently Nordic name of Gaut Biornsson. In runes that run the length of two magnificent crosses, he tells the world that he is the son of Biorn, hailing from Coll, an island in the Inner Hebrides, and advertises his own achievements as the master stonecutter of Man. "Melbrigdi, son of Athakan the smith," says Gaut on one, "erected this cross for his sin. But Gaut made it, and all in Man."

The conversion process took place as speedily among Danish Vikings in England as it did among Norwegian settlers in the Celtic lands. The *Anglo-Saxon Chronicle* recounted the conversion of the Viking warlord Guthrum as early as 878; another, Guthfrith, received a Christian funeral 17 years later and was buried in the York Minster. By the mid-10th century, cross-surmounted graves of baptized Danes filled the churchyards of England.

In some districts, this religious transformation seems to have taken place virtually overnight. In 875, for instance, the long-suffering monks at Lindisfarne finally quit their monastery on the North Sea coast and moved westward to a place of greater safety on the far side of the Pennines, a mountain range in northern England, taking with them the bones of their beloved Saint Cuthbert. A mere eight years later, they felt secure enough to return to eastern England, no less Danish in population, but now sufficiently Christian to pose no threat.

Baptism, however, could not wash away the potency of pagan myths and dreams or drive the old gods out entirely. Of the

Tendrils entwine the body of a backward-looking beast on this slab from an 11th-century Viking "box tomb," found in 1852 in Saint Paul's churchyard, London. Traces of paint on the stone suggest the animal's body was blue-black with white spots and the background was pale yellow. Runes cut into the left edge read, "Ginna and Toki had this stone set up."

many dated coins that survive from the early 900s, several bear Christian inscriptions, such as "Lord God, almighty King," while others are embossed with pagan symbols. Some carry both the sword of Saint Peter and the hammer of the war god Thor.

The fusion of beliefs was an unavoidable result of the merging of two cultures, as the newcomers, from their earliest appearance, intermarried with the local population. Consequently, many of the personalities who figure in native and Scandinavian chronicles, as well as the individuals memorialized on grave slabs in Christian churchyards, bear names that indicate a mixture of Viking and Celtic or Anglo-Saxon parentage. Inevitably, in a land visited by raiding bands and invading armies, some mingled bloodlines must have been the result of rape, but there is also evidence of amiable interaction. In fact, an English observer, John of Wallingford, accused Danish men of such underhanded foreign tricks as frequent bathing, hair combing, and the wearing of clean undergarments in order to "overcome the chastity of the English women and procure the daughters of noblemen as their mistresses."

Fighting men who had remained in the Danelaw were joined by fresh waves of immigrants who came to farm and trade. These settlers, or their children, apparently intermarried with the local population to create a new Anglo-Scandinavian stock that spoke a language in which Danish words joined or replaced the Anglo-Saxon vocabulary. At least 600 Danish borrowings—terms such as *happy, ugly, fellow,* and *ill*—entered the fledgling English language, and many thousands more found their way into local dialects that have since fallen out of use.

The placenames in this region provide their own linguistic clues to the pattern of settlement. In the eastern county of Lincolnshire, for instance, over half the names of present-day villages are of Old Norse origin. Most of the designations take one of three forms: a combination of a Norse personal name with the Old English suffix *-tun,* meaning village or farmstead; a Norse personal name with the suffix *-by,* the Norse equivalent of *-tun;* or a Norse name with the suffix *-thorp,* meaning an outlying hamlet or subsidiary settlement.

According to many scholars, words such as *Grimston* or *Colton* (the suffix *-ton* is a derivation of *-tun)* represent settlements that probably once incorporated the names of their original English owners but were subsequently renamed after conquering Danes. By contrast, terms such as *Derby* or *Selby* or any of the other 800

107

equivalents within the old Danelaw bounds indicate farmland that may never have been an Englishman's *-tun* before a Dane claimed it. Similarly, names such as Scunthorpe and Swainsthorpe denote undesirable or remote tracts of land that were still up for grabs after the well-established farms and promising new fields had been taken over.

Such settlements were never unified into a single political entity; they were held by various chieftains and kinglets, not all of whom coexisted in peace. But if the Danelaw could be said to have possessed anything resembling a capital, it was York, which in recent years has been the subject of keen archaeological interest *(pages 113-119)*. Exotic goods unearthed there—such as wine jars from the Rhineland, silk from Byzantium, and the shell of a cowrie whose only known habitats are the Gulf of Aden and the Red Sea—suggest that the city, like its trading partner Dublin, enjoyed a busy commercial traffic with foreign parts. Heaps of local and foreign coins testify to the scope of these exchanges. Included among them is an effort by some 10th-century counterfeiter to reproduce a copper replica of a silver dirhem from the mint at Samarkand, inscribed—in a faulty rendition of Arabic lettering—with a quotation from the Koran and the name of the Persian prince Isma'il ibn Ahmad.

In York and far beyond its Roman walls—which the Danes made taller by adding timber palisades—coins such as these have served as a vital source of information about the politics, as well as the economics, of the Anglo-Scandinavian world. A huge hoard discovered in 1840 at Cuerdale some 65 miles west of York, for instance, contained over 7,000 coins, all bearing dates before 903. That fact suggests that the money was hidden in that year or soon thereafter, possibly by someone on the landward stage of the trade route between Dublin and York. Many of the coins were minted in York no more than 20 years after the Danish takeover and are marked with Christian symbols, confirming the speed of the Vikings' conversion to the new faith—or their desire to impress their Christian customers. The coins are inscribed with the names of several different kings of York, including two hitherto unknown to historians.

Equally revealing are the hoards of upward of 40,000 English coins found in Scandinavia, representing only a small portion of the millions carried off at the end of the 10th century, when plundering Viking armies once again landed on England's shores—this time not just to conquer or settle but to extract tribute to swell the coffers of kings back home, as their brethren had grown accustomed to doing

The chessmen below, part of a hoard of 93 pieces found on the western shore of the Isle of Lewis in 1851, were carved from walrus ivory at a time when this area was still part of the kingdom of Norway.

108

in eastern Europe. These payments, the Danegelds, were made at sword's point, although the warriors who demanded them were as likely to be Swedish or Norwegian as Danish.

One of the raiders, Olaf Tryggvason, a future king of Norway, arrived in southeastern England in 991 with a flotilla of 93 ships. After fighting pitched battles with Saxons and plundering, he collected 10,000 pounds of silver as the price of peace and departed. Three years later, he returned to menace London and its hinterland with the celebrated Danish king Svein Forkbeard and other warriors and commanded a second, larger payment: 16,000 pounds of the precious metal, plus food for his men. Once again, the Saxons agreed to pay—but only if Olaf converted to Christianity and promised to stay away from England in the future.

Unencumbered by such a vow, Svein Forkbeard harried the English several more times during the first years of the 11th century, demanding and receiving at least 60,000 pounds more silver. Other

TRAN—SIVIT ETVENIT AD PEVENESÆ

chieftains, including the venal Dane Thorkell the Tall, arrived in 1009. Not cooperating with him carried a stiff penalty, as the archbishop of Canterbury would learn. Taken captive, he refused to let the members of his flock pay the Vikings' extortionate ransom and was brought before an evening meeting of Thorkell's men, who capped a night of drunken revelry by battering the holy man to death. "They pelted him with bones and with ox-heads," says the *Anglo-Saxon Chronicle* in 1012, "and one of them struck him on the head with the back of an axe, that he sank down with the blow, and his holy blood fell on the ground." In 1013 Svein vowed to conquer England and descended upon the island again, this time with his 19-year-old son Cnut. The Dane succeeded in chasing the king of England from the country after only a few months' warring but was not allowed to savor his victory for long. "Svein ended his days at Candlemass on February 2," the *Anglo-Saxon Chronicle* relates, "and then all the fleet elected Cnut king." An English army, however, soon forced Cnut back to Denmark, where his brother Harald had taken the throne.

Cnut returned in 1015 to wage a long campaign that culminated the next year at the battle of Ashingdon, where, according to the chronicle, "all the nobility of England" was destroyed. Having fulfilled his father's ambition, Cnut turned the kingdoms of Wessex, East Anglia, Northumbria, and Mercia into earldoms, with himself as overlord, and created a new aristocracy of Englishmen who swore loyalty to him. Then he expanded his empire, taking the Danish crown after his brother's death, claiming Norway through military action, and pressuring Scotland's king to submit to him. In a letter drafted in 1027, he could describe himself as the "king of all England, and of Denmark, of the Norwegians, and of part of the Swedes."

England, however, became the focus of his attentions. He combined the legal system of the Danes with traditional principles of English law, brought peace and a degree of unity to a fragmented

After crossing the English Channel as shown on the above section of the Bayeux Tapestry, the Norman army of William the Conqueror—a descendant of the great Norwegian chieftain Rollo—clashed in 1066 with Saxons led by King Harold Godwinson, himself the progeny of Danish and Swedish royalty. When Harold fell in combat (far left, below), the battle became a rout, as the Latin inscription concludes. It reads, "The English have turned to flight."

land, and spared no effort to become the paradigm of a Christian king. To reinforce his message to his subjects that a new day was dawning, Cnut carried out an elaborate and costly series of pious acts in penance for his ancestors' wrongdoing. He built churches—one on the battlefield at Ashingdon where his conquest was secured—showered donations on religious foundations, and transferred the murdered archbishop's body to a new resting place at Canterbury.

In 1031, to commemorate the donation of a golden altar cross to Winchester Cathedral, a church artist drew an illustration of the monarch with his left hand on the hilt of a sword and his right hand clutching a cross. Cnut died four years later, when he was only 40, and was buried in the Old Minster at Winchester, which had become his favorite royal residence. Barely 30 years after that, the Viking age in Britain would be over.

The beginning of the end occurred in Ireland as early as 968, when Brian Boru, a chieftain destined to become Ireland's king, gave the Vikings a taste of their own medicine by raiding their prosperous port at Limerick. The battle, said one contemporary chronicle, was "fierce, bloody, crimsoned, violent, rough, unsparing, implacable."

"They carried off their jewels and their best property and their saddles beautiful and foreign; their gold and their silver; their beautifully woven cloth of all colors and of all kinds; their satins and silken cloth, pleasing and variegated, both scarlet and green. They carried away their soft, youthful, bright matchless girls; their blooming silk-clad young women; and their active, large, and well-formed boys. The fort and the good town they reduced to a cloud of smoke and to red fire afterward. The whole of the captives were collected on the hills of Saingel. Every one of them that was fit for war was killed, and every one that was fit for a slave was enslaved."

Two dozen more bloody engagements followed, including the critical battle of Tara in 980, where the Irish king of Meath defeated the Viking king of Dublin, Olaf Sigtryggsson, thereby securing Irish supremacy in the region. As other native rulers shrugged off foreign domination and gradually became politically active, some aspired to take control of the entire island, leading to still more conflicts. The climax came on Good Friday in 1014, when two rival Irish dynasties—the Munster and Leinster realms—fought at the Battle of Clontarf, only a few miles outside of Dublin.

Summoned by Sigtrygg Silkenbeard, the city's king, Vikings from Scandinavia, Normandy, and other far-flung locations fought on both sides, and some 7,000 died. One of those who joined forces with the Leinster Irish, Brodir from the Isle of Man, cut down the now-aged Brian Boru, king of Munster, while he prayed in his tent. His death, however, had little effect on the outcome of the battle, which was won by the Munster army and became the subject of countless Icelandic sagas and Irish histories.

In England, the era's end came at the hands of a fresh wave of conquerors who—ironically—were of Viking stock. After Cnut, the kingdom grew weak. In September 1066 its newly elected king, Harold Godwinson, who was of Scandinavian stock, frustrated the attempts of the king of Norway, Harald Hardraade, or the Ruthless, to add England to his empire at the battle of Stamford Bridge. Three days later, however, Duke William of Normandy—a descendant of the Viking warriors who had raided and settled on the banks of the river Seine—arrived with an invasion force of his own and killed Harold at the Battle of Hastings, in Sussex, on October 14. William was crowned king of England on Christmas Day.

Historical convention has made 1066 the watershed, ending the Viking age in Britain and heralding the arrival of a French-speaking Norman ruling class that looked to western Europe instead of Scandinavia. But in other parts of the British Isles, the Norse presence would persist for much longer. Only in 1263, at the Battle of Largs, would the Isle of Man and the western-isles Scots finally displace the Norwegians, while the northern islands of Orkney and Shetland would remain in Scandinavian hands until they came to the Scottish crown as part of a royal dowry in 1468-69. Though the Vikings of the British Isles were ultimately subdued, other Norsemen survived to the west, in Iceland and Greenland, there to confront challenges as stark as any yet met.

ENGLAND'S NORSE CITY

Eleven hundred years ago Viking warriors swept across northern England, determined to seize the territory and establish a colony. Their efforts concentrated on the riverside site of present-day York, a spot occupied then by Anglo-Saxons and previously by Romans. The settlement's excellent defensive position, as well as its land and water access, made it an ideal hub for the Vikings' far-reaching network of trade and industry. On the foundations of a Roman city known as Eoforwic to the Anglo-Saxons who lived there, the Vikings established a new settlement they called Jorvik, transforming it into one of Europe's great ports and the capital of their only lasting kingdom in England. The city flourished for more than 200 years, second only to London in size and prosperity, before falling to William the Conqueror in AD 1068.

During the 1970s, modern developers targeted portions of York for massive rebuilding. Fearing for the

scientists banded together to form the Y logical Trust and set out to make a defini the areas scheduled for redevelopment. proved spectacular. Under a row of buildi oughfare known as Coppergate, a name c Old Norse for Cup-makers' Street, trust covered an unprecedented cache of Viking excavation yielded a staggering five to bones, 230,000 potsherds, and more tha dividual artifacts. Moreover, an accumula ic refuse had forestalled decay by creating ic, and oxygenless environment. The ru dwellings, shops, and warehouses, with t some walls still reaching five feet high, e the wet ground. Along with the pottery a ments common to other sites, Copperga also held arrowheads, knives, leather b textiles, a silk purse, and the ice skate ab

The partially walled city of Eoforwic fell easily to the Vikings in 866, but the following year the ousted Anglo-Saxons regrouped for a savage counterassault. "Some of them got inside," wrote a contemporary chronicler, "and an immense slaughter was made of them."

Though little has turned up from the Anglian period, an accidental discovery by York's commercial developers provided one remarkable puzzle piece. Fewer than 10 yards from the edge of the Coppergate excavation, a large mechanical digger, leveling a lot, struck a metal object. Workers assumed they had hit a piece of the demolished building, but a closer look by archaeologists revealed something different—the iron helmet of a warrior.

The headpiece proved to be seventh- to ninth-century Anglo-Saxon in origin, one of only three from this period ever found in Britain. After being subjected to computer tomography and x-rays by the Trust's scientists to determine its condition, which proved excellent, it was meticulously restored. As the scientists were removing the rust and corrosion, they revealed an inscription on the brass bands decorating the helmet. The Latin words identified the owner by the name Oshere and included a short prayer invoking God's protection. The script helped to establish the helmet's age and origin, but who the warrior Oshere was will forever remain a mystery.

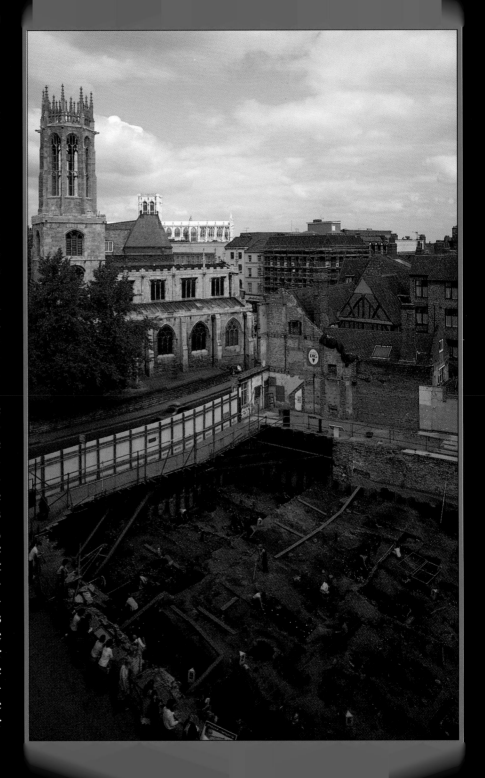

A wood-lined pit, containing pottery and other debris, held the battered helmet (right) of a soldier. Dramatic brass eyebrows and carved animal heads gave the wearer a fearsome aspect, while cheek- and nosepieces afforded his face protection. The presence of an Angian iron spearhead in the pit suggests the items were interred together, perhaps to hide them from the Vikings.

The only complete Viking-age skeleton found at Coppergate lay at the bottom of an abandoned glass furnace turned rubbish heap. The careless burial of the 25- to 35-year-old male suggests that he may well have been a casualty of war

Following the capture and successful defense of the city of Eoforwik, the Vikings turned their energies to the establishment of a prosperous trading center. As the new settlement took root, the renamed Jorvik saw a level of activity unknown since the days of the Romans. In time, the Vikings repaired and extended the city's defense works and undertook other developments. During excavation of the Coppergate area, archaeologists discovered round stains in the earth at regular intervals, evidence of wooden poles believed to have been boundary markers. Many of the property lines of modern York follow those laid out by the Vikings, making the current city a living artifact of historic town planning.

Boundaries drawn, a complex of densely packed wooden buildings rose up at the center of the city. Viking artisans often both lived and worked in these cramped quarters, resulting in a chaotic jumble of commercial and domestic life. Less concerned with sanitation than the Roman founders, they carelessly heaped trash into waste pits built close by their dwellings. This arrangement undoubtedly gave the city a pungent odor but also proved a boon for archaeologists. The diverse debris in the pits, as well as what was dropped and trampled into the earthen floors of the buildings, provided ample evidence of the residents' occupations. Remnants of raw materials and finished products alike attest to Jorvik's flourishing manufacturing industries, including woodworking, metalsmithing, weaving, cobbling and the minting of coins. Wealth engendered by commercial success created a market for imported commodities, such as Baltic amber and silk clothing, also found embedded in floors or discarded with Coppergate's garbage.

Archaeologists use white labels to mark the posts and stakes of a pair of 10th-century post and wattle buildings, once the workshops of a coinmaker and a metalsmith. Central hearths like these, ringed by limestone or tiles, were needed in both professions but could cause fires.

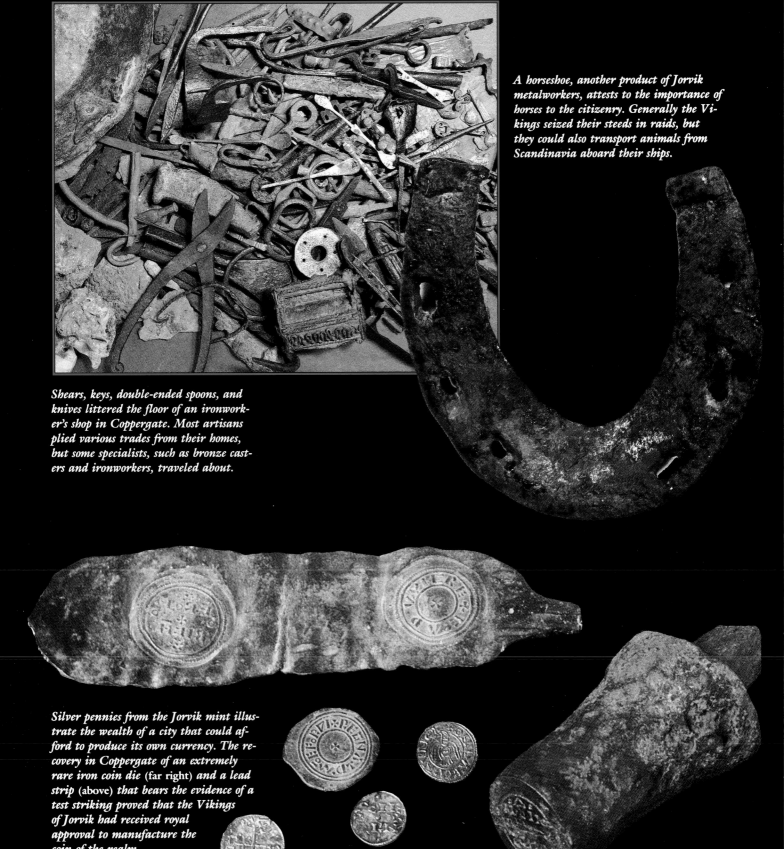

A horseshoe, another product of Jorvik metalworkers, attests to the importance of horses to the citizenry. Generally the Vikings seized their steeds in raids, but they could also transport animals from Scandinavia aboard their ships.

Shears, keys, double-ended spoons, and knives littered the floor of an ironworker's shop in Coppergate. Most artisans plied various trades from their homes, but some specialists, such as bronze casters and ironworkers, traveled about.

Silver pennies from the Jorvik mint illustrate the wealth of a city that could afford to produce its own currency. The recovery in Coppergate of an extremely rare iron coin die (far right) and a lead strip (above) that bears the evidence of a test striking proved that the Vikings of Jorvik had received royal approval to manufacture the coin of the realm.

Perhaps the most interesting of the thousands of artifacts discovered at York were the many personal effects and household items used by the Vikings in their English settlement. Though much was known previously of their prowess in both war and industry, the excavation of Jorvik gave an unprecedented glimpse of the private lives of these people.

With characteristic robustness, the Vikings enjoyed a diet notable for its variety. Huge quantities of cattle, sheep, and pig bones were found mingled with those of geese, plover, grouse, and other wild game birds. The presence of cod, pike, and herring bones and shells of various kinds indicate a fondness for seafood. The citizens of Jorvik also consumed masses of fruit, vegetables, grains, and nuts. Examining the microscopic remains of the Vikings' cesspits also revealed numbers of intestinal-parasite eggs, the product of a tainted water supply.

Fabric belonging to Coppergate residents disclosed a surprising fact about their costume. Even after cleaning, Viking textile fragments remained a uniform dull brown color. A laboratory technique called absorption-spectrometry analysis showed, however, that the cloth originally was dyed in a rainbow of brilliant hues. Evidence of a variety of dye plants appeared in all the Coppergate excavations, suggesting that dyeing was common practice. The fashion-conscious further decorated their garments with brooches, cloak pins, and ornamented belts.

The Vikings also appear to have greatly enjoyed their idle hours. Playing pieces, probably from a board game known as Hnefatafl, turned up frequently. For the more adventurous, rivers and marshes provided excellent skating in the winter months. With smoothed animal bones attached to the soles of their leather boots, skaters propelled themselves over the ice by means of iron-tipped push sticks.

Near the bank of the Foss, workers scrape the floor and wattle-lined sides of a 10th century waste pit. Archaeologists combed through an astounding 12½ tons of soil during the five-year excavation.

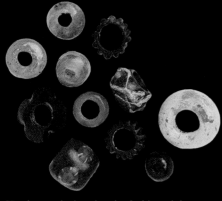

Variegated glass beads, fashioned from blocks of imported colored glass melted down at Jorvik, were probably strung between shoulder brooches.

A comb, carved from the antler of a red deer, consists of several plates held together with iron rivets. Antler was prized for its strength and flexibility.

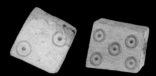

A pair of dice carved from animal bone suggests that games of chance, and perhaps gambling, were popular in Jorvik.

A rare 10th-century boxwood panpipe turned up at York. Amazingly, after cleaning, it could still be played, producing a scale of five notes from A to E.

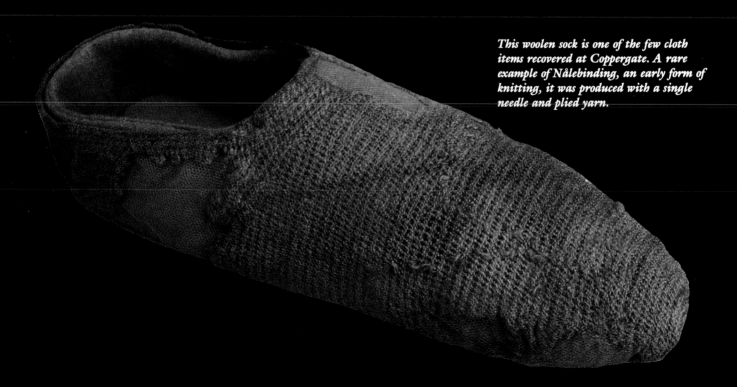

This woolen sock is one of the few cloth items recovered at Coppergate. A rare example of Nålebinding, an early form of knitting, it was produced with a single needle and plied yarn.

ACROSS THE SEA, INTO THE UNKNOWN

A deft melding of paganism and Christianity, this cast-silver amulet and pendant betrays the religious ambivalence of Iceland's settlers even after wholesale conversion of the population in 1000.

From a Scandinavian perspective, it was as inevitable as ice and the northern sun that the Vikings would sail ever farther west, past Britain and Ireland and on across the open sea to new horizons. Indeed, the Vikings envisioned a flat earth consisting of a ring of land curling around an ocean, with a still greater cosmic ocean stretching beyond the circle. They saw the terra-firma portion as broken by straits and sounds of different widths. Scandinavia, Britain, and the European continent composed part of the ring, and such North Atlantic islands as the Orkneys, the Shetlands, and the Faeroes a smaller part. It remained only for bold men with seaworthy ships and stout hearts to find the other islands that surely lurked out there. And as Europe, Britain, and Ireland had already learned, there was no shortage of seaworthy ships and bold men in ninth-century Scandinavia. While second and third sons and would-be kings ventured south and east looking for silver, land, and fame, others would travel west over the waters of the North Atlantic to gain the immortality of a good name through the risky business of exploration and, with the help of brave women, colonization.

The story of the Vikings on the North Atlantic frontier as it unfolded over the next 600 years—first in Iceland, then Greenland, and finally at the short-lived settlement led by Leif Eiriksson and Thorfinn Karlsefni in North America—is a stirring chronicle of gritty

perseverance on the edge—the edge of the Europeans' known world at the time, and in the case of Greenland, the edge of endurance and tolerance. One Greenland skeleton speaks eloquently of the fortitude required: It belonged to a poor wretch who had dislocated his shoulder; the bone had never popped back into place and yet he carried on, using his arm and wearing another socket into the scapula. Remarkably, the Greenlanders managed to survive not for a decade or a century but for 500 years amid some of the harshest, most unforgiving conditions, conditions that permitted no mistakes and conferred no amenities. To have survived at all in Greenland was an achievement; to have done so for half a millennium before Columbus made landing in the New World seems almost a miracle. But in the later Middle Ages, Iceland fell on hard times, and the Greenlanders simply vanished, disappeared in a mist that remains impenetrable today, leaving behind ruins that testify mutely to the inhabitants' existence even as they tease and tantalize archaeologists.

Dramatic vistas such as this one of Iceland's west coast greeted colonists, who were drawn to the uninhabited island by the promise of free land and a chance to escape the domination of Norway's king, Harald Fairhair. The first colonist is supposed to have arrived around 870; by 930 settlers had taken up all usable land.

Iceland, which lies at the latitude of central Norway, in good weather was only some six or seven days of sailing from a point just southwest of present-day Bergen; Greenland another two days or so beyond that. The Norse voyagers may even have had knowledge of these islands long before setting foot on them, garnered from the lore of a few intrepid Irish and Scottish seafarers. As suggested by personal names recorded in the sagas and by telltale signs on Icelandic and Greenlandic medieval skeletons, the Vikings brought with them a Celtic contingent—in the form of slaves—and may even have used Celtic oarsmen to help them get there.

The Icelandic *Landnámabók,* or *Book of the Settlements,* which was written in the early 13th century, fully four centuries after the events it describes, tells of three separate Viking navigators who within the space of a few years around 860 encountered the large, fjord-creased island with its broad green valleys rimmed by volcanoes

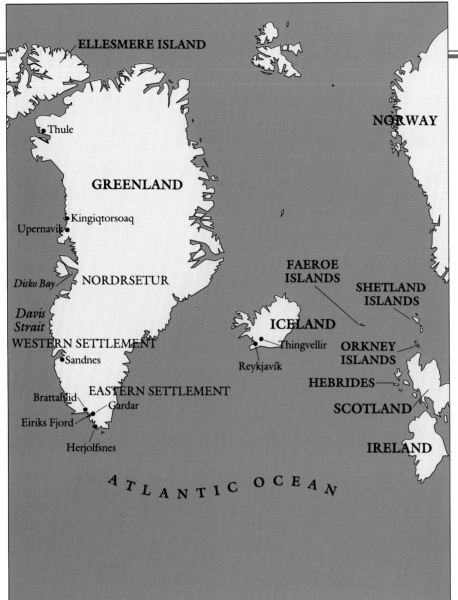

and glistening glaciers. The first two mariners, a Norwegian by the name of Naddod and the Swede Gardar Svavarsson, hove in sight of Iceland in a manner that recurs constantly in Icelandic sagas, as wind-bullied victims of capricious northern storms. Gardar wintered over and made a circumnavigation of the 3,700-mile coastline before returning home. Inspired by the tales Gardar told about this uninhabited realm, the third navigator, another Norwegian, known as Raven Floki, led a colonizing expedition to Iceland.

According to the *Landnámabók*, Floki followed Gardar's route until he reached a large fjord on the northwest coast that he chose as the site of his settlement. But Floki and company became so preoccupied harvesting the abundant animals of this arctic Eden—salmon, seal, birds—that they failed to store away enough fodder to carry their livestock through an unexpectedly long winter. When the precious imported cattle died, so did the little colony's hopes. The discouraged Floki, gazing from a hilltop at the ice that still blocked the fjord in late spring, gave the land a name that would stick—Iceland. When his party got back to Norway, some spoke more favorably of this country and its 40,000 square miles of habitable land than their failed leader. One went so far as to claim—metaphorically at least—that butter dripped from the grass in Iceland's meadows.

Scandinavian adventurers began sailing for Iceland in numbers. Such Landnámsmen, or Founding Settlers, had an unparalleled opportunity in this new land: They could claim the best steadings for themselves and their heirs, and they could name fjords and whole regions as they saw fit. And they could exploit to their hearts' content Iceland's abundant animals and its stands of willow and birch that

Vikings, primarily from Norway, used the islands to their west like stepping-stones across the North Atlantic. From the Shetlands, Orkneys, and Faeroes to Iceland and Greenland, the Scandinavians found land to settle. In addition to identifying these places, the map shows the extent of the two Viking colonies in Greenland and the sites of Eirik the Red's farm, Brattahlid, and of the Nordrsetur, the summer hunting grounds.

covered plains and valleys and extended clear up mountain slopes.

While such colonists missed the glory of the great raids and eastern trading ventures of those they left behind, through their own deeds, both good and bad, they were to leave a permanent mark on the land they tamed and on the world of letters. From their exploits came the Icelandic sagas, vivid accounts of the goings-on of ordinary men and women, as well as of kings, ghosts, and gods, that rank among the most stirring literary works of the Middle Ages. But because most of the sagas were composed, like the *Landnámabók*, long after the conversion of the Vikings to Christianity and were shaped by the knowledge and personal agendas of the saga writers themselves (many eager to flatter those people claiming descent from the protagonists), none can be trusted for factual accuracy, and many were clearly written as fantasy.

Today, archaeology, bioarchaeology (which uses biological samples to reconstruct the lifestyles of long-dead people), and paleoecology (which involves the reconstruction of past environments) are both challenging and confirming the picture of the Viking age in the North Atlantic. Some questions apparently clearly answered by the accounts now seem more open than once thought. The integration of the old stories with the growing body of excavated evidence is a major challenge to researchers at work in the region. The sagas say, for example, that the first settlement was founded around 870, near present-day Reykjavík, by a Norwegian called Ingolf Arnarson. Recently, the Icelandic archaeologist Margret Hermanns-Audardottir has disputed this. She claims that a Scandinavian-style farm that she has excavated on Heimey in the Westman Islands off Iceland's south coast predates Ingolf's arrival by some 200 years, and she offers radiocarbon dates as proof of her claim. Although these dates have been disputed, a Viking settlement somewhere in Iceland earlier than Ingolf's remains a possibility.

Other archaeological finds seem to confirm some of the traditions underlying the Ingolf and Floki stories. Digging in downtown Reykjavík, Iceland's capital, at a site known by the address Tjarnargata 4, archaeologists have laid bare the remains of at least one early farm now much cut up by hot-water pipes and foundations. Radiocarbon dates put the farm in Ingolf's day. More than 65 percent of the animal bones recovered from the midden, or refuse heap, of the first owners have been identified by the scientists as coming from birds whose nesting colonies would have been easy pickings for

TALES THAT SING OF VIKING FEATS

Locked in a vault behind a two-ton door in the basement of the Manuscript Institute of Iceland resides the country's greatest treasure—an assortment of handwritten manuscripts. They are Icelandic sagas that were collected by Danes in the early 18th century and for years were housed in Danish libraries. In 1971, under pressure from Iceland, the Danes returned the epics. When the first installment arrived in Reykjavík harbor, Icelanders joyfully crowded the wharves to greet the manuscripts' homecoming.

It is little wonder that the Icelanders were pleased to get their sagas back, for these narratives are Iceland's supreme artistic achievement. They were recorded between the 13th and 14th centuries by Christians, yet they extol the exploits of pagan heroes who undertook daring expeditions in the 10th and 11th centuries. The finest ones resound with eternal truths. Fate is master, but when human beings encounter their destinies, they can be heroic and

prove themselves to be worthy of remembrance.

Recited at festivals, weddings, and other gatherings, the sagas were passed orally from one generation to the next. They were immensely popular in an age of few entertainments. As literacy spread, families eventually had the tales written down on calfskin vellum with the quill feathers of swans or geese, dipped in ink made from bearberry juice. They were then read and copied by poor farmer and wealthy landowner alike, becoming heirlooms that proudly reminded their owners of the deeds and exploits of ancestors.

Akin to historical novels, sagas are based on facts but laden with romance and adventure. Historians once found the stories credible sources, but today, while they still regard the sagas as a wonderful way to view Viking society from the inside, they tend to weigh the content against mounting archaeological evidence of what life was really like in the saga age.

Viking King Olaf Tryggvason is shown below slaying a wild boar and vanquishing a sea ogress. The pictures illustrate an epic based on Olaf's actual exploits, inflated to mythic proportions. They are found in the Flateyjarbok, *a collection of Icelandic sagas.*

hunters before the flocks learned to fear the Viking interlopers. The bones of the now extinct great auk were among those found, suggesting that the flightless species was particularly vulnerable.

Walrus bones from Tjarnargata 4 tell a related story. Some of them belonged to immature animals that were probably killed on nearby pupping beaches. Were the contemporaries of Ingolf harvesting local walrus herds? And since no native walruses survive in Iceland today, did the first Icelanders contribute to the eventual local extinction of the beasts? In any case, it seems clear that the colonists did encounter the natural bounty that so distracted Floki and that like later European settlers in similarly virgin lands, they set about consuming it as fast as they could.

Land was for the taking, at least in the beginning. Even after real-estate laws came into existence, a man could still claim as his own all the territory that he could cover on foot in a single day carrying a lighted torch. The *Landnámabók* reported that a woman was entitled to as much land as she could travel while leading a two-year-old heifer, "in good condition on a spring day between the rising and setting of the sun."

In the absence of adequate timber—Iceland's trees were badly stunted—the homesteaders built their houses out of sod. Excavations have shown that the earthen walls were frequently three to six feet thick, a necessary protection against the icy winter winds. The main rooms sometimes extended 40 to 100 feet in length and, like the long houses of Scandinavia, were heated by hearths running down the middle of an earthen floor.

As the colony grew larger, the need for a ruling body became apparent. But resolved to be "free of kings and criminals," as one of the settlers put it, the colonists set out to govern themselves, through regional assemblies led by local chiefs. In 930 the most powerful chieftains united to establish the Althing. This countrywide body was in fact western Europe's first parliament and the closest approximation to a self-governing republic since ancient Rome. The Althing consisted of a council of 36 (later 48) chiefs called *godar,* literally "godly ones," who maintained their positions by protecting and representing their regional subjects in exchange for their fealty.

The Althing met annually in June, following the spring stock roundups, at Thingvellir, a site on a plain about 30 miles from Reykjavík. Delegates brought their retinues and erected "booths," or living quarters, in what amounted to a VIP campground. They so-

cialized and transacted business in between sessions of gathering at the cliff called the Law Rock and listening to the reading of the Icelandic legal code (one third was read each year), hearing lawsuits, and considering new laws and amendments, including, in AD 1000, the adoption of Christianity. The delegates elected a president who served a renewable three-year term, but he lacked the power to enforce laws; that was up to the individuals affected, a weakness that would ultimately prove fatal to the Icelandic commonwealth.

The elaborate legal code known as the Gragas, or Gray Goose, named after its binder's color, prescribed terms of settlement for the feuds that continually erupted among high-status Icelanders, established regional things and courts, and set forth the penalties miscreants could expect. For theft the punishment was hanging or beheading, misbehaving slaves were whipped or mutilated, while a person convicted of witchcraft would be stoned, drowned, or "sunk in a morass." A form of exile called "outlawry," in which an offender was deemed legally "unfit for all help and shelter" and condemned to a period of wandering, was a particularly sobering sanction. In some cases payment or atonement could mitigate a penalty.

Through diligence and hard work settlers with good land prospered, and the island's economy initially flourished. In addition to wool, Icelanders were soon exporting such commodities as cheese,

Lava cliffs surround the natural arena of Thingvellir, site of the annual Icelandic assembly meetings that began in 930. Part legislative session and part country fair, the event featured a recitation of the republic's legal code. The speaker, with his back to the assembly, faced the cliffs directly under the two-pronged outcropping, so that his voice might reverberate off the stone wall and be heard by all. One of the earliest written versions of the code extant (right) *dates from 1260.*

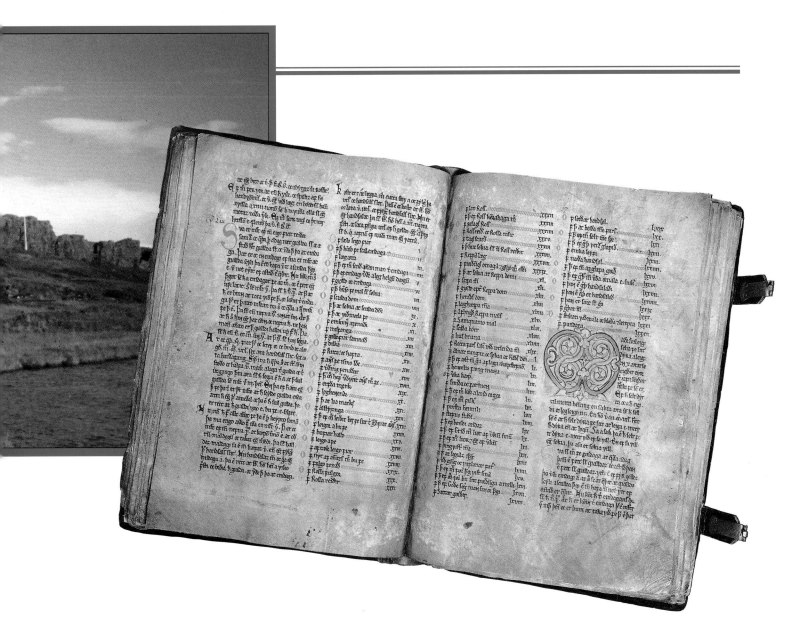

tallow, salted fish, and the falcons coveted by European and Arabian princes, receiving in turn such necessities as timber, metals, tools, flour, tar, malt, and honey.

There were early signs, however, of trouble to come. The settlers, it seems, were not husbanding their resources as well as they might have. Their worst mistake was the careless destruction of the soil. "They lived like prodigals," the Welsh Nordic historian Gwyn Jones writes, "destroying the protective birch scrub by intensive grazing, firewood felling and accidental forest fires." They also cut the trees for charcoal, used in the smelting of bog iron, a thick, low-grade ore, and turned the metal into tools and into the nails that they needed for shipbuilding and for boat repair. Analyses of pollen layers at archaeological sites show that the forests that were there when settlers arrived were quickly felled, and the shallow soil began to erode not long afterward.

At Svalbard, a farmstead in northeast Iceland dating to the 11th century, Thomas Amorosi, an anthropologist from Hunter College in New York, has made discoveries similar to those of Tjarnargata 4 but spanning some 700 years. During this long period of occupation, four broad categories of animal bones dominated the top layers of the refuse pile—cattle, caprines (sheep and goats), fish, and seals, but in the lower, earlier layers, bird bones made up 25 percent of the finds. Amorosi

Godafoss, one of Iceland's most beautiful waterfalls, made even more spectacular by the lava rocks in its midst, received its name (Waterfall of the Gods) at the time of the Christian conversion. It was at this spot that a pagan priest denounced his heathen beliefs and cast his idols into the raging currents.

interprets the shifting ratio of cattle to caprine remains, with the relative numbers of cows declining, as indicative of a greater emphasis on wool production and perhaps a decline in good pastureland, which in turn suggests to him overgrazing and possible erosion. An increase in seal bones, in middens such as the one at Svalbard, several hundred years after the founding of the colony tells scientists that smaller farms were falling on hard times and landholders had to supplement their diets by hunting sea mammals. Remains of shellfish, which Icelanders normally disdained, are an even stronger indicator of lean economic times.

What cause for optimism the Icelanders may originally have had was soon dashed. Not only was all of the good farmland taken up, but the population had swelled to perhaps 50,000 to 60,000 people, putting pressure on the available resources. Then, midway through the pre-Christian era, in the decade of the 970s, catastrophe struck: A terrible famine afflicted the island. During the most desperate of the famine years, the saga account says, "men ate ravens and foxes and some men had the old and helpless killed and thrown over the cliffs. Many starved to death, while others took to stealing, and were condemned and put to death for it." As a direct result of the famine years, people living in the more marginal areas began to look beyond Iceland for new opportunity, and an individual soon emerged who would lead the next phase of the relentless Viking advance across the northern sea.

Eirik Thorvaldsson Raudi—known as Raudi, or the Red, for his fiery red hair and beard—was someone who seemed to be in a perpetual fury. At least in his early years in southwest Norway and then in Iceland, Eirik was forever exploding in murderous rages with the result that he was sentenced to punitive banishment three times before he was 35. On the first occasion he and his father, Thorvald, were exiled from their native Norway after what the sagas cite matter-of-factly as "some killings." In about 970, with Eirik just out of his teens, the family migrated to a rocky, unpromising section on the northwest Iceland coast. Eirik married the daughter of a well-to-do family and moved to better land near his inlaws' property, but before long he was chest deep in trouble again. The saga account says that Eirik's serfs started an avalanche that crushed a neighbor's house. The neighbor's kinsmen killed the serfs, Eirik slew the kinsmen, and soon afterward Eirik was banished for a second time and forced to move 50 miles away to the Breidha Fjord district.

Here Eirik graciously loaned his house beams—timber had become so precious that he had dismantled his house—to a new neighbor named Thorgest while Eirik sought a site for a new farm. The rub came when Eirik demanded the return of the beams and Thorgest declined to give them back. This was not an attitude that Eirik suffered gladly, so he and a detachment of men went to Thorgest's house and reclaimed the beams. Thorgest took umbrage, and when the feuding families met in combat, Eirik killed two of Thorgest's sons. The case was brought to the local assembly, where Eirik was found guilty of "lesser outlawry." The sentence was three years' exile from Iceland. The year was 982.

Eirik had a notion where he wanted to go. Some 50 or 60 years earlier a sailor named Gunnbjörn had happened upon land about 450 miles west when his ship had been storm blown off course between Norway and Iceland. Gunnbjörn was not tempted to go ashore—the land looked bleak and uninhabitable—but word of his discovery got around. In the time before he was to begin his sentence, Eirik bought a knorr, loaded it with supplies, and persuaded some of his followers to try their luck with him in looking for the place Gunnbjörn had sighted.

Traditional 11th-century Scandinavian foliage art sets off a portrayal of Christ as a shepherd with haloed saints or apostles on two of a series of carved pine wall panels. The panels, originally created for an Icelandic church, survived over the centuries as recycled roofing material in local farmhouses.

Buttercups dot a hollow that marks the site of a long house dwelling at Eirik's farm. Livestock wintered in barns with narrow stalls (inset), where a whale's scapula forms a partition.

A glacier discharges icebergs into Greenland's Eiriks Fjord, named for Eirik the Red, who established a farm nearby. A contemporary account tells of men climbing the mountains to scout for ice-free land, "but nowhere have they found such a place, except what is now occupied."

The adventurers sailed west in the summer of 982, most likely coming in sight of Greenland after six or seven days. On reaching the icebound, uninviting east coast, presumably close to the 65th parallel, Eirik turned south and tracked along the shore until he rounded Cape Farewell at the southern tip. Northwest of the cape he came abreast of the first site that looked promising, an area of long, blue-green fjords reminiscent of Norway's, with rich grass and even wildflowers growing on their banks. Eirik wintered on an island and explored the fjords the following spring and summer.

No one recorded Eirik's musings, but he might well have thought that this was a place with pastureland as good as that in Iceland. If he and his men investigated carefully during their three summers in Greenland, as they probably did, they would have found beaches piled high with accumulated driftwood borne there on arctic currents from Siberia, edible berries, and emerald fjord-side fields. They might have seen seal, caribou, and possibly polar bears, and it would have been easy for the men to catch fish in the fjords and streams. Eirik might even have been serious when he named the country Greenland, "arguing," as the saga account reports, "that men would be drawn to go there if the land had a good name."

Eirik returned to Iceland in 985 and commenced organizing an expedition to colonize Greenland. By spring of 986 he had put together a formidable company of 25 shiploads of Icelanders, the whole fleet numbering perhaps 700 people, along with their livestock and possessions. Unfortunately the voyagers were assaulted by a ferocious storm and 11 of the 25 ships in Eirik's expedition either sank or turned back in the violent seas; the remaining 14 made it to the fjords with about 400 settlers.

Eirik became in effect the chief of chiefs in the colony; the outlaw had survived to rule. He and his family established a farm they named Brattahlid—Steep Slope—on the choicest piece of real estate, hard by a body of water that not surprisingly would be named Eiriks Fjord. Other colonists claimed the grasslands bordering the numerous fjords and carpeting the valleys between them, creating a ribbon of occupation that extended about 120 miles at the site on the south coast that came to be called the Eastern Settlement.

At least three smaller fleets of colonists arrived over the next 14 years, by which time the Eastern Settlement was well on its way to its eventual total of 192 farms, and a second colony, known as the Western Settlement, was flourishing 300 miles up the southwestern coast. Ninety farms would ultimately operate there, and the population of Viking Greenland would level off at 5,000 to 6,000.

At roughly the same time Eirik and his colonizers were getting established, yet another storm-tossed Viking seafarer was making yet another accidental discovery. The Icelander Bjarni Herjolfsson had returned to Iceland from a trade voyage to Norway only to learn that his father had joined Eirik's band in Greenland. Bjarni set sail for Greenland, but fog and storms drove him past the southern coast and eventually in sight of a low-lying, wooded land. Since this landfall looked nothing like the description of Greenland he had been given, Bjarni spurned the pleas of his crewmen to go ashore and instead sailed north along this strange coast and then east, where he finally found Greenland and his father.

Curiously, the news of Bjarni's discovery failed to inspire Eirik or any other Greenlanders to follow up, at least not immediately. They may have been too busy establishing their farms, or the next chapter may have been awaiting the right hero. At any rate, 15 years elapsed before Eirik's son Leif, who had demonstrated his

can Archaeology in 1948-49 established that the trench dug for the foundation contained colonial-era pottery, glass, clay pipes, and a gun flint and fixed the tower's construction in the 1600s.

A runic inscription purportedly discovered among the roots of a tree near Kensington, Minnesota, has inflamed imaginations since surfacing in 1898. The so-called Kensington stone is a 30-by-15-inch slab inscribed with runes and a date of 1362. Though the town has made a major tourist attraction of the stone, analysis of the writing reveals not only that its language is a mixture of Swedish and Norwegian found only in the American Midwest but also that its carver used a hardware-store-variety chisel with a one-inch bit.

Authentic Viking artifacts have been identified at various North American sites, however. A Norse penny, minted between 1067 and 1093, turned up in a Maine Indian camp. Archaeologists came across bits of cloth, chain mail, and other fragments of iron and copper while working in arctic Inuit villages. Though such finds may represent trade goods, an Inuit-carved wooden figurine from Baffin Island of a Norseman indicates probable face-to-face contact. Confirmation in the 1960s of a Norse settlement in Newfoundland heightened the expectations of Viking scholars, but no other large-scale finds have yet materialized. The discovery on a Danish beach in 1992 of shells belonging to New England steamer clams that were carbon-dated to the 13th century suggests the mollusks may have been brought there by Vikings or clung to ships as larvae before being deposited in the water where they matured.

seamanship in a series of voyages between Greenland and Norway, decided to find out what Bjarni had seen. Leif Eiriksson, described in one of the sagas as "big and strong and the most excellent man to look at," may also have wondered whether timber or furs were available in the new land. Leif bought Bjarni's ship and sailed around 1000 with a crew of 35. Attempting to follow Bjarni's route in reverse, he moved down the North American coast until coming to a spot deemed hospitable enough for a winter camp, believed to have been the northern tip of Newfoundland. Leif stayed only until the following summer, but before he left he planted the seed for one of archaeology's longest-running controversies by naming his settlement Vinland, meaning Land of Grapes *(pages 147-157)*. The *Greenlanders' Saga* reports that Leif not only found grapes but brought them back to Greenland—though northern Newfoundland is well north of grape-growing country.

Eirik the Red, who would have made the voyage himself but for a broken leg, died soon after Leif returned to Greenland, and with Leif now obliged to stay home, command of the next expedition passed to his younger brother Thorvald. The saga says Thorvald stayed two winters and explored the coast before the Norsemen had their first, inevitably fatal, encounter with North American natives. The Vikings called them Skraelings, which means Wretches or Savages; they were probably Algonquin Indians. Thorvald's men killed several Indians they found asleep under skin boats, and in a subsequent clash Thorvald himself was slain with an arrow. The Norsemen buried him and sailed home.

The third and final Viking expedition to the New World chronicled in the sagas was mounted a few years later by the Icelander Thorfinn Karlsefni. This time the Norse, intent on settling, came in three ships and brought livestock. Stopping first at Leif's camp, they then sailed south to a sheltered site, with good pastureland, that they called Hop, where they found natives willing to exchange furs for milk and cloth. But the amicable relations soon deteriorated into hostility again, and the Norse headed home after three years.

The Greenland pioneers whom Leif Eiriksson rejoined on his return from Vinland had created a viable community of small cattle and sheep ranches on the narrow strip of grazing land located at the edges of the icecap. They lived in houses made of turf and stones, roofed with sod-covered driftwood. A fully endowed Greenland farm might boast a dozen buildings, including byres, or cow barns, and even saunalike bathhouses.

Digs at Brattahlid, beginning in the 1930s, show that the farm originally owned by Eirik supported about 50 cows as against 10 to 20 at an average-size farm. Archaeologists inferred the size of the herd from the number of stone-walled stalls in the byres. The cattle were small—probably the size of a healthy Great Dane—and kept in dark, airless stalls all winter, at the end of which they were so enfeebled that they had to be carried to the pastures.

Greenland sheep were a small, sturdy breed with less fleece but with the crucial capacity to survive a cold climate. A study done in Iceland by the archaeologist Karen Marie Christensen of Denmark's Aarhus University, based on data from Icelandic farms, concluded that 9 sheep, or alternately 6 sheep and half a cow, were needed to support a man for a year; a family of six thus required perhaps 50 sheep.

The excavation of a cemetery next to Greenland's oldest Christian church yielded 144 Viking-age burials. After Greenland's conversion to Christianity, large-farm owners often erected churches on their property. The earliest, at Brattahlid, is known as Thjodhild's Church after Eirik the Red's wife.

The Brattahlid excavations also helped sketch a more intimate portrait of the Greenlanders. An examination of 155 skeletons from the farm's cemetery—possibly including those of Eirik the Red and Leif Eiriksson—showed that several of the men stood over six feet tall. Twenty-three of the 52 males were between 40 and 60 at death, while 17 were from 20 to 40. Of the 37 skeletons identified as female, three were past 60, 12 between 40 and 60, and another 14 from 20 to 40. Their teeth were worn but otherwise healthy, and most of the older people seemed to suffer from arthritis.

The cause of death was apparent in only a single case—a man in his thirties had been stabbed in the chest with a large, wood-handled knife, which was still in the grave. A recent reexamination of the Greenland skeletons yielded evidence that such violence was no aberration; an appalling number of wounds and fatal injuries were apparently the result of sword and ax.

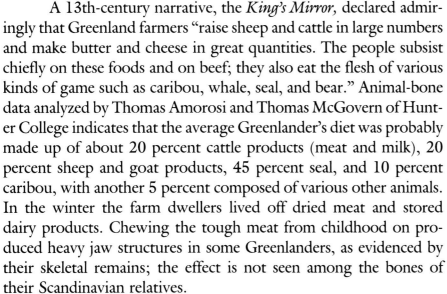

A diagram of the cemetery at Eirik's farm reveals the usual pattern of early Christian burials, with most of the men interred south of the church, most of the women (red) to the north, and a majority of the children to the east—the direction in which all bodies were laid. Above, an anthropometrist, who studies the dimensions of the human body, prepares a skull for measurement.

A 13th-century narrative, the *King's Mirror,* declared admiringly that Greenland farmers "raise sheep and cattle in large numbers and make butter and cheese in great quantities. The people subsist chiefly on these foods and on beef; they also eat the flesh of various kinds of game such as caribou, whale, seal, and bear." Animal-bone data analyzed by Thomas Amorosi and Thomas McGovern of Hunter College indicates that the average Greenlander's diet was probably made up of about 20 percent cattle products (meat and milk), 20 percent sheep and goat products, 45 percent seal, and 10 percent caribou, with another 5 percent composed of various other animals. In the winter the farm dwellers lived off dried meat and stored dairy products. Chewing the tough meat from childhood on produced heavy jaw structures in some Greenlanders, as evidenced by their skeletal remains; the effect is not seen among the bones of their Scandinavian relatives.

Greenland middens have also yielded bones of arctic foxes and wolves (probably hunted for their fur) and hares. Herds of caribou were apparently channeled by means of strategically placed stones and cairns to cliffs and driven over the lip. The absence of any harpoon discoveries suggests that harp seals, taken during the spring and summer migration, may have been hunted similarly, herded into shallow water or toward shore to be slaughtered. The Norse apparently never learned to hunt ringed seals, common in Greenland waters in winter, by zeroing in on their breathing holes and harpooning them as Inuit, or Eskimo, hunters still do.

"Whatever comes from other lands," the *King's Mirror* said, "is high in price, for this land lies so distant from other countries that

135

men seldom visit it. And everything that is needed to improve the land must be purchased abroad, both iron and all the timber used in building houses." But Greenlanders were not without goods to offer in exchange: wool and hides, fox and bear pelts, a tough rope that was made from walrus hides, the narwhal tusks known as "unicorn horns" in Europe and prized for their presumed magic powers, walrus ivory, seal oil, butter and cheese, and the beautiful gyrfalcons that were so cherished in European courts.

The Greenlanders obtained many of their most lucrative export items on summer trips to the hunting grounds known as the Nordrsetur, around Disko Bay on the west coast. From the Eastern Settlement, this was a round-trip journey in six-oared boats of 50 days, 30 from the Western. Some hunters apparently ventured even farther north. One of the more remarkable finds in Viking Greenland was made more than a century and a half ago. In 1824 an Inuit found three stone cairns on an island six degrees north of the Arctic Circle at latitude 73 degrees north. A small, flat rune-stone, broken off at less than five inches, was set inside one of the cairns. It read as follows: "Saturday before the minor Rogation Day (April 25), Erling Sighvatsson and Bjarni Thordarson and Eindridi Jonsson erected these cairns and . . ." The rest of the message is missing. The date was established as early in the 14th century. If the three hunters were that far north in late April, they had probably wintered in the vicinity.

A danger-filled expedition such as this to the frozen far north may well have had a purpose broader than the hunt. Walrus and polar bear figurines, probably worn as amulets, have been found on Greenland farms, and walrus and narwhal skulls have been discovered buried in churchyards. McGovern infers from these finds that the far north and its animals may have been the stuff of legend and mystery, "the center of a rich tradition of saga spinning and semi-Christian magic, whose vestiges we can only dimly perceive in the scattered archaeological finds." Then again, if the Greenlanders still believed in

136

a land ring around a central ocean as their ancestors had, they may have been looking for a polar route to Norway.

In their remote country, the Greenlanders needed whatever help they could get merely to survive. Just getting there could be harrowing. The sagas are awash in tales of shipwrecks, strandings on forlorn shores, and desperate treks over drift ice. One tale chronicled the 12th-century disappearance of two ships in a storm and the discovery of the seamen's remains four years later beside an east-coast fjord; two men lay outside, with axes nearby, the others were in a makeshift hut. A man known as Corpse Lodinn was said to have made a living gathering up the bodies of luckless mariners such as these, boiling the flesh off their bones, and bringing the skeletons back to the settlements for proper burial.

As they did with so much else, Greenlanders looked to Iceland as the model for their political system. In the early years Althing delegates met at Eirik's farm; when the Latin Church later established its seat at Gardar, between two major fjords in the Eastern Settlement, the once-a-year conclaves moved there. One story has Leif Eiriksson bringing Christianity to Greenland at the behest of the Norwegian king, adding that Eirik heatedly rejected the idea—though his converted wife had a small chapel built on their land. The first permanent bishop arrived in 1126 following a gift-laden visit to Norway by Greenlander Einar Sokkeson, who presented the king with furs, walrus tusks, and a live polar bear. The Church soon became a major force in Greenland life, erecting a small cathedral at Gardar, with 12 churches in the Eastern Settlement and four more in the Western Settlement available to worshipers. By the mid-1300s the Church owned or controlled roughly two-thirds of the best pasture-land in the country, and the cattle

A finely worked length of wood featuring the carved heads of three felines and a dragon that surfaced in the Western Settlement resembles ornamented chair arms pictured in medieval paintings and seals. The Viking carving style suggests that it dates from the earliest days of Greenland's colonization.

herd at Gardar was even larger than that at Eirik's farm, though there were occasional priestly complaints that the independent-minded Greenlanders were "difficult" and even "cantankerous."

As farmers and stockmen, the Greenlanders were as ecologically careless as the Icelanders, but in Greenland the odds against the land recovering were much higher. The early settlers cut down the willows and birches that grew near the fjords for firewood or perhaps to allow more space for grass for their livestock. But the animals prevented the plants from regenerating, and the arctic wind finished the job by tearing away the unprotected vegetation that remained. Hilly sites eroded, and sand drifted over many level fjord-side pastures. Archaeological pollen profiles show that willow or alder pollen present prior to the Norse arrival in Greenland vanished in the ensuing centuries and reappeared only after the Viking colony died out.

A land where nature was more temperate might forgive such mistakes, but in Greenland soil reserves were too skimpy and the growing season too short, especially after the climate cooled during the Little Ice Age, which began in approximately 1250 and did not end until 1850. The drop in temperatures had less effect on the Inuit people who had migrated to Greenland from North America, crossing the northern ice, at about the same time that the Vikings arrived from the other direction. For the most part the Vikings and the Inuit avoided each other. The Inuit lived farther north and on the coast, close to the seals that they depended on. Neither culture seems to have had much impact on the other one. But sometime around 1300 the Inuit established their presence on Disko Bay, in the heart of the area where the Norse conducted their annual hunts. However warily, Inuits and Norsemen must have encountered each other as they competed for game. They may have met more frequently as the Inuit moved south, which they did around this time. They may even have lived fairly close to each other; the sagas recount a few instances of friendly contact.

But by the mid-14th century Norse-Inuit relations had apparently soured. King Magnus Eriksson of Norway called for a military expedition against the Greenland heathens in 1355, and though his summons went unanswered the implication was that violence had broken out. An entry in the Icelandic annals for 1379 says that Skraelings killed 18 Greenlanders and abducted "two swains and a bondswoman" that year. Though no archaeological evidence for any serious clash has yet surfaced, an Inuit folktale tells of a series of

GREENLAND'S ISOLATED CHURCH

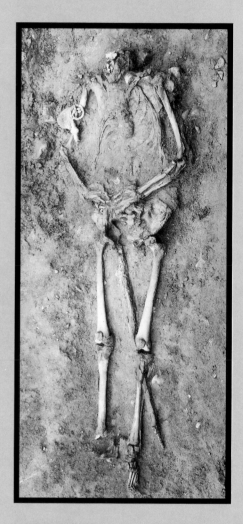

After the Norse settlers of Greenland converted to Christianity in the early 11th century, at least 16 parish churches cropped up in the settlements. Attracting bishops to the outpost was difficult. But there were benefits for those who braved the journey. Excavations at Gardar, the bishop's see, reveal that the episcopal estate comprised a large farm and a house with a hall able to hold hundreds of people. A stone cathedral, dedicated to Nicholas, patron saint of seafarers, arose on the Gardar plain and boasted glass windows instead of animal gut skin, a luxurious touch.

Customarily, clerics were laid to rest under the floor of the cathedral. The accouterments of one burial, discovered during excavation of the north chapel, left no doubt about the occupant's station. An episcopal ring, missing its stone (presumably a sapphire to ward off temptations of the flesh), graced the skeleton's right hand. That same hand clasped an ash crosier, or bishop's staff, with a crook of carved walrus ivory. Archaeologists put the bishop's burial date at around 1200, corresponding with the death of Bishop John Smyrill in 1209. Records show that during his tenure in Gardar, Smyrill visited his friend, the bishop of Iceland, who reportedly employed a female sculptor named Margarethe. Perhaps the crosier, a rare and beautiful work of art, was a gift presented from one bishop to another. Eventually, such gains, whether spiritual or material, must not have seemed enough to warrant living in Greenland, for after 1378 bishops received appointments to the post but never went.

skirmishes ending in the burning of a band of Norsemen inside a church. Such tales are especially problematical because of their lack of any time context. The full story of Norse-Inuit contacts during the colony's later years remains tantalizingly out of reach.

In Iceland, which had no native peoples to contend with, the Norse had only themselves to blame for the long decline that began not long after the pre-Christian age ended in the 11th century. The absence of any enforcement arm in the government had given regional chiefs the de facto power to maintain law and order. By the 11th and 12th centuries the number of local potentates had dwindled to perhaps a half-dozen men who commanded private armies they hurled at each other in an unending series of dynastic wars. When they were not fighting one another, the Icelandic lords were scheming to gain ascendancy within their clans; murders were as common as betrayals and shifting alliances. Meanwhile, the yeomen farmers who had pledged their loyalty to a chief in exchange for protection became more like peasants yoked to a European fief.

Between 1262 and 1264 the feuding chiefs of Iceland made submission to the throne of Norway. Peace ensued, but so did economic stagnation. Norway was just beginning a period of economic decline brought on by the ascent of the Hanseatic League, the alliance of German trading cities that thrived between the 13th and 15th centuries. The result was a short-term increase in Icelandic trade followed by a long silence from a Norway now in the economic doldrums. Icelandic farmers were forced to abandon their land, householders became tenants, and beggars roamed the countryside.

Natural calamities compounded Iceland's travail. Declining temperatures increased the number of bad ice years, and the 13th and 14th centuries brought an appalling succession of plagues—hundreds are thought to have died in a 1301 epidemic—famines, volcanic eruptions, and earthquakes. The sagas chronicled the catastrophes—the "cattle death year" of 1200, the "sand-winter" of 1226 (probably due to ash from an eruption), "many severe winters at once" in the 1280s, causing numerous deaths from starvation, "the great livestock death winter" of 1291. In 1300 the volcano Hekla erupted with an accompanying rumble of earthquakes. Another volcanic outburst in 1362 was described by a historian as "in all probability the biggest explosive eruption in Europe since Pompeii."

Epidemics broke out three times in the decade of the 1380s. Archaeological evidence supports the grim-times tales in the sagas. The number of both seal bones and shellfish found in digs on Icelandic farms shows an increase during the later Middle Ages, a sign that ranching was suffering.

The increase in drift ice that came with the lower temperatures of the Little Ice Age had even graver consequences in Greenland. The *King's Mirror* described pack ice extending so far out to sea from the coast that it took four days or more to walk across it. The Greenlanders yielded their independence to Norway in 1261—a year before Iceland did—in exchange for trade concessions, but the ice-clogged shipping lanes as well as increasing competition for their trade goods, from Russia for hides and furs and Britain for woolens, left Greenland isolated. Norway, which now had a monopoly of the Greenland trade, gradually faded as a presence in the distant territory as its maritime prowess ebbed and plague struck its population, reducing it by perhaps as much as half. The cargo ships that had called regularly now came only rarely; the last documented official trade voyage from Norway to Greenland was in 1367. The Church likewise abandoned the province; no bishop was sent there after 1378. Europeans had long thought of Greenland as perched on the edge of the world. By the 14th century it seemed to have dropped off.

Sometime before 1350 the first phase of what would become the grand conundrum of Viking history took place: The Norse men and women who lived in the smaller and more isolated Western Settlement—perhaps as many as a thousand—vanished, disappeared as abruptly and conclusively as Greenland receded from European consciousness. Ivar Bardarson, a Norwegian priest, journeyed from the Eastern Settlement that year in order to discover what had happened to them and arrived to find "never a man," the account of his voyage says, "either Christian or heathen, merely some wild cattle and sheep." Bardarson's crew loaded what animals they could aboard their ship, and the priest reported that in his opinion Skraelings now held the settlement.

The mystery persists, despite archaeological efforts to resolve it. The finds at a farm excavated in the 1970s by Claus Andreasen and Jens Rosing of the Greenland Museum only add to the unanswered questions. Andreasen and Rosing uncovered several rooms of a farm building. Animal bones found in the room that served as a larder spoke eloquently of the plight of occupants of the house. "Perhaps this last year," writes Thomas McGovern, who served as zooarchae-ologist at the dig, "was not the ordinary sort of year." Winters were becoming progressively harsher. Stored cheese might have run out, and the family might have turned in desperation to food they disdained in more generous years, such as hare and ptarmigan.

"Slowly the farmer would begin to kill off his domestic stock, the sheep and goats first as they were less valuable," McGovern speculates. If the spring thaw was late, the pregnant cows and ewes may have delivered young that the family was forced to eat rather than put out to pasture. Finally, the cattle themselves were killed and butchered, the whole herd probably going into the larder. Without stored milk and cheese, the family could not hope to survive the next winter.

"The remains of no human bodies were found," McGovern goes on. "Instead, the limb bones of a hunting dog lay there, its skull in the larder and its pelvis in the main room beside the fire." One leg bone bore knicks of a knife. Was the family at last compelled to eat their dog? Did they eventually pack and leave? Where could they go?

A second farm in the Western Settlement, investigated in the early 1990s by Andreasen and Jette Arneborg, would indicate sudden abandonment. In the sand-filled house they found the remains of a weaving room, complete with a large wooden loom, still holding an unfinished length of woolen cloth. Other artifacts recovered include a double-edged comb, soapstone vessels, an iron knife, and arrows made from reindeer antlers.

What happened to the inhabitants of the Western Settlement? How could so many people disappear without a murmur? According to a church account written in the 17th century, the bishop who ordered Bardarson's trip believed that the Greenlanders had "joined themselves with the people of America" (which meant the Inuit); he thought they had gone native. But clearly some evidence for such an unlikely, late-in-the-game assimilation would have surfaced if that were true. Other theories abound: The Skraelings wiped the colony out; a plague or famine decimated the population; they were done in by infestation of caterpillars that consumed the foliage; they emigrated en masse to Vinland. (But in what ships? Their original vessels had rotted, and they lacked wood for new ones.) They tried to emigrate

The hood and cloak of this 600-year-old Inuit wooden figure from northern Greenland mark it as a portrayal of a Viking. To the smaller Inuit the Norse must have bulked huge. Skeletons show that the men averaged 5 feet 7½ inches tall and were heavily muscled.

DENYING THE COLD REALITY: EVERYDAY CLOTHING IN GREENLAND

Throughout the 19th century, visitors to Cape Farewell, Greenland's southernmost point, reported finding human bones, pieces of coffins, and bits of textiles on the beach of the former Viking port of Herjolfsnes. Fragments continued to appear, and in 1921 a Danish scientific commission ordered an excavation. Hitting frozen ground, the Danes feared nothing would be left of the cemetery, but as the exposed soil thawed their excitement grew. The earth apparently had hardened shortly after the interments, and this had helped preserve the clothes in which the dead had been buried.

The scientists spent five weeks carefully removing the woolen garments from the ground, packing them in brook moss to keep them moist before they were sent to Copenhagen. When the clothes were examined, they spoke movingly of the hard existence of the Greenlanders: They were patched and worn. Uniquely, the Herjolfsnes burials offered a look at an entire collection of the garb of ordinary citizens of the 13th to the 15th centuries.

One revelation described by expedition leader Poul Nørlund was that the clothing bore "not one trace of adaptation to the Arctic climate, not a single intrusion from the Inuit culture." The Greenlanders had dressed in a European style that was recognizable from paintings of the medieval period; despite their isolation, they were still fashion conscious.

The most extraordinary find was the array of hoods with a liripipe, a tail-like streamer hanging from the crown that could be wrapped around the neck. This was "the headdress of Dante and Petrarch," Nørlund wrote, "as it is Robin Hood's." These clothes, he went on, "make the Norsemen live for us more than any find of household utensils, implements, or weapons could do."

The liripipe hood (below) *represented the height of fashion in 14th-century Europe. A seemingly indispensable garment, a gentleman wore one even when meeting the pope and a sheep thief while hanging on the gallows, as illustrated in an Icelandic legal document* (right).

Most of the 30 woolen robes recovered at Herjolfsnes resemble the dress at left, identified as a child's because of its size. Apparently, men, women, and children wore pullover garments with rounded necklines, fitted at the waist, often with insets that produced flaring skirts (below). An exception is a shorter man's coat fastened with buttons (right). Undergarments consisted only of hose.

Archaeologists leave intact a cruciform-shaped area to preserve the chronological strata in an excavation of the Western Settlement's so-called Farm Beneath the Sand. Completely covered over by shifting sands, the outcome of erosion, this farm and others seem to have been suddenly abandoned for reasons apparently unknown even to the inhabitants of the older Eastern Settlement.

but perished in their small boats in the angry Greenland Sea. Did the colder, stormier, and longer winters finally kill the people off? (But not the animals?) Again, it seems impossible that there would be no record detailing such a catastrophe. Contemporary historians and archaeologists are without an explanation.

The Eastern Settlement and its 3,000 or 4,000 residents hung on for at least another 70 years and perhaps that many years more, but then they too faded into the northern mists. A shipload of Icelanders, driven off course in a storm, turned up there in 1406. For reasons unknown—possibly heavy pack ice—they remained four years. In that time they witnessed two ceremonies, the burning in 1407 of a man convicted of seduction by means of black magic—which suggests that the old pagan ways had either reasserted themselves or had never entirely disappeared—and a wedding on September 16, 1408. When the Icelanders finally returned home, they signed declarations that the wedding had been lawfully performed, hence the documentary record of their visit. Their departure from the Eastern Settlement in 1410 is the last verifiable evidence of Norsemen in Greenland. After that, only silence.

A papal letter from 1492 lamenting the likelihood that Greenlanders had abandoned the faith notes that "no ship has sailed there for the last 80 years." Excavation in the 1920s of a graveyard at a spot called Herjolfsnes, once a port of call for trading ships coming from Norway, revealed burials dating as late as the 15th century. The archaeologists were surprised to find that the corpses had been buried in clothes that were not just European in style, but fairly up-to-date in cut, revealing the Greenlanders' failure to adjust to the changing climate and adopt warmer Inuit garb *(pages 142-143)*.

By 1540, when an Icelander ironically named Jon Greenlander stopped in Greenland, the colony was deserted. The seaman sailed into a fjord where he found booths and stone houses and the body of a hooded man—the last Norseman in Greenland?—lying face down on the ground. Subsequent expeditions persisting into the 18th century came up empty in their search for Norse survivors.

The discovery in the 1930s of a mass burial site at Unartoq in the Eastern Settlement fueled speculation that a 1401 epidemic may have drastically reduced the colony's population. Or it could have been a clash with the Inuit, or something else. An Inuit folktale recorded in the 18th century suggests another speculative explanation: pirates. German and English pirates are known to have raided Iceland in the 15th century, and Greenland was even more vulnerable (if less accessible). The tale collected by Niels Egede, a Greenlander who set down his conversation with an Inuit shaman, tells of a great pirate fleet disgorging buccaneers who "fought with [the settlers], plundering and killing." When the pirates returned a year later, the

The stone church of Hvalsey, the best preserved of Greenland's Viking ruins, was the setting for the last recorded ceremony in the colony. Marooned Icelanders witnessing a wedding there in 1408 of one of their party to a Greenlander reported when they got home that many people had attended, yet by 1540 the Eastern Settlement was totally deserted. After four years' absence in Greenland, one of the men found that his wife, thinking him dead, had remarried.

Inuit took some of the Norse women and children to their camp, but when the Inuit went back to the settlement they saw that "everything had been carried away, and houses and farms were burned down." Despite extensive archaeological investigation of various farm sites, no archaeological finds have yet corroborated this otherwise plausible story.

The descendants of Eirik the Red and his band of pioneers had scratched a livelihood for 20 generations from this unforgiving, forsaken, tempest-tossed outpost on the fringe of civilization, "the world's end," as the pope's letter of 1492 called it. And they did so while remaining Vikings to the last: never assimilating, never adapting in the slightest to the accommodations the natives who shared the country with them had made. Had they adapted, had they hunted seal with harpoons and clothed themselves in bear furs and sealskin, given up their farms when erosion and climatic change made them untenable and shifted to hunting, would they have lasted longer?

Thomas McGovern thinks so. The Norse in Greenland "showed a dangerous lack of resilience," he writes. In adversity they dug in rather than change, displaying a "single minded conservatism" that ended in their extinction, whether it was slow and agonizing or sudden and catastrophic. "While the Norse colony waned and died," he points out, "the Inuit hunters spread and prospered." Why this fatal failure to adapt?

McGovern suggests that the powerful religious and landowning interests "profited from a system that made elaborate religious ceremony and cattle-keeping marks of status." To adopt Inuit ways would have been to embrace heathenism and give up identification with things European. The elite had a stake in the status quo. "In the long run," McGovern concludes, "too much cultural stability may be as deadly as too little. A society led by court-appointed bishops, lonely for the comfort of the European homeland, may have found itself a poor match for a society led by accomplished hunters whose ancestors had conquered the high Arctic."

It is the richest kind of irony to view the end of the Greenland drama, and with it the end of the grand, lusty chronicle of seamanship and adventure and plunder, conquest, and finally colonization—the end of the Vikings—as the pale payout for a failure to adjust, an inflexibility that seems at once stubborn and timid.

IN SEARCH OF VINLAND

For the better part of a millennium, the Vikings' 11th-century expeditions to North America's eastern shore were largely forgotten. Within the opus of Scandinavian lore, their daring was celebrated primarily in two tales—*Greenlanders' Saga* and *Eirik's Saga*. Yet, as historians were quick to concede, the seafaring Norse could scarcely have avoided contact with the New World. Since 800, Norwegian colonists plying the northern seas had ventured ever farther west. Greenland, which they settled in 986, lay only 200 nautical miles from the North American continent, across the narrowest portion of the Davis Strait.

Leif Eiriksson knew of the existence of this land from an account by a seafarer who, driven off course by a storm, had sailed along its coast. Son of Greenland's founder, Eirik the Red, Leif set off in search of it with a crew of 35 around the year 1000. Steering a southwesterly course, he soon put in at a promontory where, the saga relates, a river flowed out of a lake. A grassy meadow stretched from the sea to a wood, and grapes grew in the area. Leif named the land Vinland for "the good things they found in it" and built "big houses."

Publication in the early 1800s of the *Greenlanders' Saga* and its companion tale, *Eirik's Saga,* sparked a flurry of Vinland research. Most scholars, intent on the sagas' talk of wild grapes, concentrated their search in more southerly regions of North America's eastern seaboard, such as Rhode Island and Cape Cod. The 20th-century Norwegian explorer Helge Ingstad focused instead on the sagas' nautical leads, on ancient maps, and on his instincts about where a Norseman would feel at home. In 1961, after nearly a decade of investigation, Ingstad, his wife, archaeologist Anne Stine, and a party of excavators boarded the *Halten (above)* in Montreal and headed down the St. Lawrence for Newfoundland. There, on the island's grassy northern tip, near the village of L'Anse aux Meadows, the remains of a Norse settlement awaited. Ingstad would call it Vinland.

The sagas provided clues to Vinland's location: On the way there, goes the story, the voyagers encountered a barren, flat expanse, with glaciers as a backdrop, that they named Helluland, or Flatstone Land; and a vast forest they called Markland, or Land of the Woods. The similarity between Helluland's glaciers and Baffin Island was not lost on Ingstad, who also noted how like Markland's wooded coast the shores of Labrador are. Leif—who navigated by coastline—would have met both lands en route to Newfoundland.

More telling still were the sailing times reported for the voyage. When recalculated using the actual distance from place to place—assuming the six-knot speed typical of Viking vessels—the times coincided nearly perfectly with those given in the sagas.

Ingstad also scoured old maps for clues. Both the Skálholt *(below)* and Resen maps, which may be copies of ancient Icelandic ones, located Vinland on a peninsula whose shape and latitude strongly suggested northern Newfoundland.

Even so, most scholars remained dubious, insisting that Vinland, which they read as "Wineland," had to be much farther south. But Ingstad, who knew that Viking homesteaders valued good pastureland over grapes, reasoned that perhaps the Vikings had quite another meaning for Vinland that had no connection with grapes. He construed "vin" as having an old Nordic meaning, "meadow."

In 1960 Ingstad switched from books and maps to fieldwork. By boat and plane he scouted North America's coastal regions for ruins. For months, his efforts turned up nothing. Then he met George Decker, a fisherman who lived in L'Anse aux Meadows. Decker escorted Ingstad across sweeping pastures to a bluff, where he pointed to the faint earthen tracings of house sites. Ingstad had a distinct feeling of recognition. Surely, he thought, Leif had made his camp here.

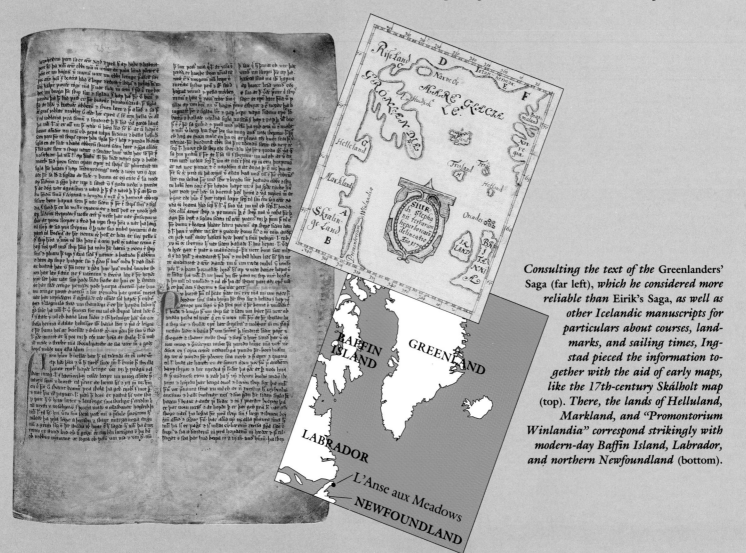

Consulting the text of the Greenlanders' Saga *(far left),* which he considered more reliable than Eirik's Saga, *as well as other Icelandic manuscripts for particulars about courses, landmarks, and sailing times, Ingstad pieced the information together with the aid of early maps, like the 17th-century Skálholt map (top).* There, the lands of Helluland, Markland, and "Promontorium Winlandia" correspond strikingly with modern-day Baffin Island, Labrador, and northern Newfoundland (bottom).

Seated aboard the Halten, Ingstad and his wife, Anne Stine, confer over a sea chart. Ingstad, a lawyer by training, left his practice in 1926 to become an arctic explorer. In 1953 he journeyed to Greenland to study the old Norse ruins there before setting out to trace the Vikings' New World exploits.

Ingstad strolls a stretch of the 40 miles of beaches north of Cape Porcupine, Labrador. He believes them to be the Marvelstrands of the sagas. According to Eirik's Saga, the Viking voyagers called them Marvelstrands because, "it was such a long business sailing past them."

149

*Reduced to a hillock, the Norse settle-
ment—seen near the excavators' tents
in the middle distance—commands a
strategic view of Epaves Bay. North-
ward lies an island where, says the
Greenlanders' Saga, the voyagers first
went ashore and found "dew upon the
grass," which they tasted, saying "they
had never known anything so sweet."*

*While George Decker looks on, Ingstad
(second from left) and helpers sift the soil
for finds. Among the most important relics unearthed were, clockwise from upper
left, a bone-needle fragment; a needle
hone; a ringed bronze pin; and a soapstone spindle whorl.*

In June 1961 Ingstad and a team of archaeologists led by Anne Stine returned in the *Halten* to L'Anse aux Meadows. The ruins lay atop a beach terrace spanning either side of Black Duck Brook, which—like the river of the sagas—emptied into a bay that contained salmon.

After setting up their camp, the crew members went to work on a small house site. At the building's west end, Anne Stine uncovered a stone fireplace and a slate-lined ember pit, where coals were banked for the next day's fire. Anne Stine knew that design well; she had seen an identical hearth at Leif Eiriksson's farm in Greenland.

Over the next six years, the Ingstads unearthed the remains of seven more buildings. Each one of them comprised a spacious hall, or *skali,* and a smaller outbuilding. From the blackened traces of turf walls, postholes, and piles of collapsed roof sod, the excavators determined that the structures had been built of turf. Some of them had been large, measuring up to 70 feet in length and capable of sheltering between 50 and 100 people.

Each skali was heated and lit by one or more fireplaces. Packed soil on both sides of one such hearth indicated the presence of benches, perhaps sleeping platforms.

A small but telling cache of artifacts confirmed the settlement's Norse origins. In what was designated Hall F, diggers found an Icelandic stone lamp or base of a door pivot and a soapstone spindle whorl for spinning yarn, which indicated the presence of women. Other discoveries included a ringed pin of bronze for fastening a Viking cloak, and a bone needle with a drilled eye *(below, left)*. Strewn throughout the sites were iron rivets and quantities of slag—a byproduct of the smelting of iron.

Evidently, a smith skilled in the fine Norwegian art of extracting iron from bog ore had numbered among the voyagers. His smithy, complete with stone anvil, was later discovered across Black Duck Brook from the house sites. Close by was a peat bog, from which the raw material for the smithy had come—lumps of bog iron.

Excavation reveals how sod walls once divided the 70-by-55-foot Hall F into several rooms. The spindle whorl and needle hone (left) were found here.

The bog's marshy flats, from which the iron ore came, also served as a dumping ground for the community. Archaeologically, they would prove a gold mine. In 1973 the Canadian Parks Service began excavations there under the direction of archaeologist Bengt Schonack and completed them under Birgitta Wallace. With the help of local fishermen, excavators stripped away the sedge to reveal the Norse cultural layer. Tannic acid in the bog acted as a preservative, presenting diggers with a number of interesting discoveries. The choicest find was a small plank that may have served as a repair patch for a boat *(below)*. Also recovered were a thousand or so fragments of wood—debris from trimming wood.

According to Wallace, these discards suggest that much of the labor performed at L'Anse aux Meadows was dedicated to boat repair. A survey of the site's iron artifacts bears this out: Nail fragments differ in composition from the iron produced at the settlement, indicating that the nails from which they came were made elsewhere and removed during boat maintenance. The settlement's scanty iron yield—only six pounds as calculated from the weight of the smelting slag—would

have been enough for only 100 replacement nails.

One castoff bit of wood offers still more clues to how the Vikings spent their days here. Among the shavings, archaeologists discovered three butternuts and the burl of a butternut tree that had been worked with a metal instrument. Wallace believes that the burl and the nuts—native only to more southerly climes—were brought north by the settlers during exploratory expeditions into the Gulf of St. Lawrence, although Ingstad claims that the nuts could just as well have been left by Indians.

Intriguingly, the northern limit of butternut trees corresponds to that of wild grapes. Since grapes have never been native to Newfoundland, Wallace asserts that the sagas' stories of grapes—as well as the name Vinland—derive from the voyagers' contact with the gulf. Vinland, says Wallace, is not L'Anse aux Meadows, but a New World region to which Leif's settlement is only the gateway.

A treenail of pine still protrudes from a patch that may have once been affixed to a Viking boat. The plank was scrapped because of its irreparable split. A rope of spruce roots (far right) found near the plank may have lashed the board to the ribs of the hull.

Outfitted in rubber overalls, excavators bail water from trenches that have been cut in the bog turf. Pollen analyses of core samples taken from the site reveal that the bog was even wetter 1,000 years ago when the Vikings tapped it for bog ore and tossed their offal into its oozy depths.

A blaze burns in the central long hearth of reconstructed Hall A. Wooden doors opened onto four rooms arranged end to end. At dusk, some 30 people returned to the cozy chambers to gather on the benches and trade stories over the evening meal. The same platforms sufficed for beds.

Held together with pegs, green willow twigs, and tanned seal strips, the timber framework of the reconstructed houses awaits sodding. Native timber, culled from the forest near the site, was used in the building process.

While scholars continue to debate whether L'Anse aux Meadows is indeed Leif Eiriksson's Vinland, few question its Viking identity. In 1978 the UNESCO World Heritage Convention recognized it as the first authenticated Norse settlement in North America and named it a World Heritage Site.

That same year, on plots adjacent to the excavations, the Canadian Parks Service began facsimile reconstructions of the three buildings nearest Black Duck Brook.

As these *(left)* show, the sod walls and earthen floors belie the comforts the dwellings afforded. The great halls housed the gentry and their helpers, attested by a glass bead and a gilded ring fragment found within the area of Hall D. Outbuildings, which were warmed by hearths and rimmed with benches on which to sit, doubled as workshops and sleeping quarters for slaves.

All were structures built to last. But from the sparse finds and absence of graves, archaeologists have surmised that the Norse occupation was short-lived. The sagas hint that hostile Skraelings drove the settlers away. Perhaps it was so: Excavations reveal that at least five indigenous American peoples inhabited L'Anse aux Meadows before and after the Vikings.

A door such as this would have greeted Leif Eiriksson 1,000 years ago when, after an afternoon's hunting, the ruddy chieftain returned bearing a clutch of eider-duck eggs for his dinner.

Wood-framed smoke holes tilt skyward atop the grassy roofs of reconstructed Hall A (behind) and Houses C (center) and B (far right). Slaves assigned to the smith may have resided in Houses B and C, where traces of roasted bog ore and lumps of smelting slag indicate ironworking.

MAKERS OF SEABORNE HISTORY

The peoples of Scandinavia described a unique historical arc. Beginning as farmers, tilling the limited arable land of Sweden, Denmark, and Norway, some of them early became adept at overseas trade. Then suddenly about AD 800 many went "a-Viking," raiding and looting in the British Isles, in western Europe, even in today's Turkey—before settling down once again to cultivate the soil and build towns not only in their own native region but also in the many places they had conquered and colonized.

Key to the momentous shift from farming to trading to raiding was the perfection in the eighth century of the fast, double-ended, square-rigged Viking ship. Ideal for surprise attacks, each vessel could carry 30 or more warriors across stormy seas to launch devastating assaults. Combined with superb seamanship, the swift boats enabled the Vikings in their heyday to dominate from Ireland in the West to the Volga River in the East.

The Viking era is generally said to stretch from about AD 800 to 1100. But Scandinavian traders were well known around the shores of the Baltic Sea and in northern Europe as far back as Roman times. And Viking history extends beyond the conventional 1100 date in Iceland and Greenland, where Vikings settled and carried on their northern ways in relative isolation. In a sense, Viking history continues today, living on in the customs, laws, placenames, and bloodlines of the people in the many parts of the globe to which the Norse ventured more than a millennium ago.

THE·PRE-VIKING AGE
AD 5-800

SWEDISH WARRIOR'S HELMET

In the year 5, a Roman fleet reached Denmark's Jutland Peninsula, making the first contact between the world's greatest power and the Scandinavian people who were the Vikings' ancestors. The Norse, the historian Tacitus wrote, already had oar-propelled ships with prows at both ends and were fierce warriors.

Inspired by such contacts with Europe, Norse merchants were soon setting forth from their lands in crude cargo ships to trade silver fox and other fine furs, walrus-tooth ivory, and Baltic amber for silks and spices coming from Asia via Rome, wine and glassware from the Rhineland, and other luxury goods from a variety of locales. With the collapse of the Roman Empire in the fifth century AD, Europe was convulsed with wars as Germanic tribes battled for territory, yet Norse traders continued to operate through this so-called Migration Era (400-600), bringing new wealth to Scandinavia.

This period was followed by what is often referred to as the Vendel era (600-800), named for an archaeological site in Sweden full of evidence that the warrior elite led opulent lives and were equipped with the finest arms and armor, such as the bronze and iron helmet shown above.

WESTERN EUROPE
AD 800-1100

GOTLAND PICTURE STONE

The year Charlemagne was crowned king of the Franks, 800, also marks the time when the Vikings were about to become terrors of the European continent. In 810 they made their first recorded attack there, hitting the northern coastal area called Frisia, and they returned to pillage the rich Frisian trading town of Dorestad between 834 and 837. Heavy attacks on France began in 841, the Vikings sailing up the Seine and Loire valleys, which were ill-protected by Charlemagne's successors, to sack Rouen and in 842 to plunder the walled town of Nantes. Paris came next, a large force attacking the city in 845. At about the same time, a Viking fleet sailed southward from enclaves they controlled on the French coast to raid towns in Spain, including the great Moorish stronghold of Seville. By 859 Vikings had sailed past Gibraltar to attack ports in southern France and Italy. The onslaught continued, especially on France, through the 870s, until in 911 King Charles the Simple ceded to the savage Norse the province that would bear their name, Normandy.

In their many campaigns, the Vikings often sailed near their targets, then rode horses on land operations, as shown in the ancient stone above that pictures both a ship and a mounted warrior.

A MOVE TO THE EAST
AD 800-1100

BRONZE BUDDHA FROM INDIA

THE BRITISH ISLES
AD 800-1100

VIKING PENNY FROM YORK

ATLANTIC OUTPOSTS
AD 860-1540

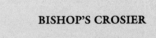

BISHOP'S CROSIER

Perhaps as early as the year 550 Danish and Swedish merchants began heading east across the Baltic to trade furs and feathers, walrus ivory, and slaves with the people of what would become Latvia and Russia. Over the years, they brought back increasingly exotic goods from their excursions down Russia's rivers to the Black Sea area and even into Asia, as attested by the Buddha above. The merchants were followed in the 800s by Viking warriors who sailed the Dneiper and the Volga southward, fighting and looting as they went. In 860 a large Viking force in 200 ships stormed the greatest prize of all, Constantinople. Other Viking bands returned to the city, with pillage and profit in mind, in 907, 941, and 944. Before then, warring Slavic tribes in northern Russia had, in 862, begged a Viking chief named Rurik and his brothers to rule over them and bring peace. Rurik obliged and founded the Scandinavian dynasty that would rule Russia until the time of Ivan the Terrible's son in the 16th century. In 882 Rurik's successor Oleg extended his rule to Kiev and by the close of the 900s the Rus, as the Norse were called, held sway from Lake Ladoga in the north to the Bosporus.

The first recorded Viking raids hit England in 793, when the Norse plundered the priory on the tiny British island of Lindisfarne, and in 794, when they looted the abbey at Jarrow. Ireland was next, Vikings making the first of many attacks on Irish monastic centers in 795. Hit-and-run raids on English and Irish towns and religious communities continued into the 840s, but starting in 851 large invasion forces began thronging ashore—and often settled down to establish permanent bases. By 880 the Vikings controlled most of England, only the southwestern kingdom of Wessex being free of their domination. Power center for the Vikings was York, where they struck their own coins, such as the penny bearing a sword and the hammer of Thor above.

In the 900s Irish kings fought the interlopers until, by the late 11th century, the island was largely free of Viking domination. In England, though, the Norse continued to exert control. The Danish king Svein Forkbeard invaded afresh in 994, and in 1015 Svein's son Cnut returned, defeated an English army at the battle of Ashingdon and became king of England. Finally in 1066 came the great invasion by the Normans—originally Vikings themselves—who defeated King Harold at the Battle of Hastings.

Viking navigators may have seen Iceland earlier than is thought, but the first to lead a colonizing expedition there was a Norwegian, Raven Floki, in AD 860. Floki's colony apparently did not last, the first permanent settlement being planted about 870 by Norwegian Ingolf Arnarson. The colonists survived and even prospered and in 930 founded the Althing, western Europe's first parliament. In 1000 Iceland converted to Christianity; one of the island's bishops doubtless owned the bronze crosier head above, found at the site of the Althing.

Colonists trying to settle the grassy shores of Greenland's fjords were less fortunate. The island was first sighted in 982 by Eirik the Red who, having been banished from Norway, was exiled once again, from Iceland, for killing two men. Returning to Iceland in 985 he recruited an expedition and set sail with his followers in 25 ships, only 14 of which survived storms and reached Greenland, where two colonies were established. Around the year 1000 Leif Eiriksson sailed westward from Greenland, landing in North America and setting up a temporary camp. For unknown reasons, Greenland's so-called Western Settlement was abandoned in 1350; 100 or so years later, the original Eastern Settlement was also mysteriously abandoned.

ACKNOWLEDGMENTS

The editors thank the following individuals and institutions for their valuable help in the preparation of this volume: Peter Addyman, Archeological Research Centre, York; Gerald Bigelow, Bowdoin College, Brunswick, Maine; Michelle P. Brown, British Library, London; Johan Callmer, University of Umea, Sweden; Canadian Parks Service, L'Anse aux Meadows, National Historic Site, Newfoundland; Helen Clark, Society for Medieval Archeology, Woodbridge, Suffolk; Birthe Clausen, Viking Ship Museum, Roskilde; Joachim Herrmann, Berlin; Wendy Horn, Manx Museum, Isle of Man; Helge Ingstad, Oslo; Ingmar Jansson, University of Stockholm, Uppsala; Eirik Irgens Johnsen, University Museum of National Antiquities, Oslo; Andrew Jones, Archeological Research Centre, York; Katie Jones, Archeological Research Centre, York; Christian Keller, University Museum of National Antiquities, Oslo; Jónas Kristjánsson, Stofnum Arna Magnussonar, Reykjavík; Emma Kublo, Novgorod State Museum, Novgorod; Terje I. Leiren, University of Washington, Seattle; Poul Mørk, The National Museum Copenhagen, Copenhagen; Evgieny N. Nosov, Institute of the History of Material Culture, The Russian Academy of Sciences, St. Petersburg; Raghnall O'Floinn, National Museum of Ireland, Dublin; Gudmundur Olafsson, National Museum of Iceland, Reykjavík; Julian Richards, University of York, York; Anna Ritchie, Royal Museum of Scotland, Edinburgh; Else Roesdahl, Aarhus University, Moesgaard, Denmark; Elena Rybina, Moscow State University, Moscow; Ian Tait, Shetland Museum, Scotland.

PICTURE CREDITS

The sources for the illustrations that appear in this volume are listed below. Credits from left to right are separated by semicolons; credits from top to bottom are separated by dashes.

Cover: © University Museum of National Antiquities, Oslo. Background C. M. Dixon, Canterbury, Kent, England. End paper: Art by Paul Breeden. 6, 7: © Husmo-foto, Oslo. 8: © University Museum of National Antiquities, Oslo. 11: © Nordbok, Gothenburg, Sweden; © University Museum of National Antiquities, Oslo (2). 12, 13: Background Werner Forman Archive, London/Statens Historiska Museum, Stockholm. The Royal Library, Copenhagen—Mauro Pucciarelli, Rome—Werner Forman Archive, London/Statens Historiska Museum, Stockholm. 15: Art by Time-Life Books. 16, 17: © University Museum of National Antiquities, Oslo. 19: Werner Forman Archive, London/Upplandsmuseet, Uppsala, Sweden. 20, 21: Per-Olof Bohlin/Uppsala University Institution for Archaeology, Museum for Nordic Antiquities, Uppsala, Sweden—drawing by Allan Fridell, photographed by Olle Lindman/Uppsala University Institution for Archaeology, Museum for Nordic Antiquities, Uppsala, Sweden—Olle Lindman/Uppsala University Institution for Archaeology, Museum for Nordic Antiquities, Uppsala, Sweden (2). 22: © University Museum of National Antiquities, Oslo. 23: © Mittet Foto, Oslo—© University Museum of National Antiquities, Oslo. 24, 25: © Tromsø Museum/University of Tromsø, Norway—art by Fred Holz (2). 26: © Historical Museum/University of Bergen, Norway. 27: Photo: Lennart Larsen, © British Museum Publications Ltd., London. 28: Bengt A. Lundberg, A.T.A., Statens Historiska Museum, Stockholm—art by Fred Holz. 29: Bengt A. Lundberg, A.T.A., Statens Historiska Museum, Stockholm. 30: Gabriel Hildebrand, A.T.A., Statens Historiska Museum, Stockholm—Werner Forman Archive, London/Statens Historiska Museum, Stockholm. 31: Gabriel Hildebrand, A.T.A., Statens Historiska Museum, Stockholm. 32: Chris Schwarz/Maclean's. 33: Art by Time-Life Books—courtesy Gaia Foundation, Oslo. 34: © University Museum of National Antiquities, Oslo. 35: © National Board of Antiquities/The National Museum of Finland, Helsinki. 36, 37: © University Museum of National Antiquities, Oslo; courtesy Christian Keller, Oslo. 39-49 Background Morten Gøthche, Viking Ship Museum, Roskilde, Denmark, from *Les Vikings . . . Les Scandinaves et l'Europe, 800-1200,* Association Française d'Action Artistique, Ministère des Affaires Etrangères, et Auteurs, 1992. 39: Inset Viking Ship Museum, Roskilde, Denmark. 40, 41: Map by Time-Life Books; Viking Ship Museum, Roskilde, Denmark (2). 42, 43: Viking Ship Museum, Roskilde, Denmark. 44, 45: Viking Ship Museum, Roskilde, Denmark, from *Five Viking Ships from Roskilde Fjord,* by Olaf Olsen and Ole Crumlin-Pedersen, The National Museum, Copenhagen, 1978; Viking Ship Museum, Roskilde, Denmark—Viking Ship Museum, Roskilde, Denmark, from *Five Viking Ships from Roskilde Fjord,* by Olaf Olsen and Ole Crumlin-Pedersen, The National Museum, Copenhagen, 1978. 46, 47: Viking Ship Museum, Roskilde, Denmark. 48: Archiv für Kunst und Geschichte, Berlin/Viking Ship Museum, Roskilde, Denmark. 49: Foto Kit Weiss, The National Museum, Copenhagen. 50: Gabriel Hildebrand/Riksantikvarieämbetet, Stockholm—Archive J. Herrmann, Berlin, Foto K. Hamann, from *The Northern World,* Harry N. Abrams, Inc., New York, 1980 (coins). 52, 53: Jan Norrman/Riksantikvarieämbetet, Stockholm. 54, 55: Photo: Lennart Larsen, Statens Historiska Museum, Stockholm, © British Museum Publications Ltd., London. 56: Werner Forman Archive, London/The National Museum,

160

Copenhagen. 59: Jan Norrman/ Riksantikvarieämbetet, Stockholm; art by Fred Holz, from *The Vikings*, by Else Roesdahl, Allen Lane The Penguin Press, 1991, © Else Roesdahl—Jørgen Grønlund, Copenhagen. 61: © University Museum of National Antiquities, Oslo. 62: Map by Time-Life Books, based on maps from *The Viking World*, by James Graham-Campbell, published by Frances Lincoln Ltd., London, 1980/*The Viking*, Nordbok, Gothenburg, Sweden, 1975. 64: G. P. Skachkov, The State Hermitage, St. Petersburg, Russia. 65: Novgorod State Museum, Novgorod, Russia (2)—G. P. Skachkov, The State Hermitage, St. Petersburg, Russia. 66: Länsmuseet i Gävleborgs Län, Gävle, Sweden. 67: Gabriel Hildebrand/Riksantikvarieämbetet, Stockholm—Gianni Dagli Orti, Paris. 68, 69: Jim Brandenburg/ Minden Pictures—G. P. Skachkov, The State Hermitage, St. Petersburg, Russia. 70, 71: Gabriel Hildebrand/ Riksantikvarieämbetet, Stockholm. 73: Church of Nea Moni, courtesy Editions d'Art Albert Skira, Geneva. 74: Foto Kit Weiss, The National Museum, Copenhagen. 75: Jim Brandenburg, © National Geographic Society. 77: Werner Forman Archive, London/Statens Historiska Museum, Stockholm. 78: © University Museum of National Antiquities, Oslo. 79: Werner Forman Archive, London/ Statens Historiska Museum, Stockholm; photo: Lennart Larsen, Statens Historiska Museum, Stockholm, © British Museum Publications Ltd., London. 80, 81: © Nordbok, Gothenburg, Sweden; Foto Kit Weiss, The National Museum, Copenhagen. 82: The Royal Library, Copenhagen—Claus Hansmann, Munich/Helms Museum, Hamburg. 83: C. M. Dixon, Canterbury, Kent, England. 84: Aalborg Historical Museum; Claus Hansmann, Munich/Statens Historiska Museum, Stockholm. 85: Claus Hansmann, Munich/Universitetets Oldsaksamling, Oslo. 86: C. M. Dixon, Canterbury, Kent, England. 88, 89: Lindisfarne Priory/English Heritage, London; Werner Forman Archive, London. 91: Maps by Time-Life Books. 92: Kungl. Biblioteket, Stockholm/MS A.135, ff.9v-11. 94: Photo: Lennart Larsen, Historical Museum/University of Bergen, Norway, © British Museum Publications Ltd., London. 95: Photo: Lennart Larsen, © British Museum Publications Ltd., London. 96: The British Library, London; *The Irish Times*, Dublin (2). 98, 99: York Archeological Trust Historical Picture Library, York, England. 100, 101: Copyright British Museum, London. 102: Royal Commission on the Ancient and Historical Monuments of Scotland, Edinburgh. 104: C. M. Dixon, Canterbury, Kent, England. 105: © Historical Museum/University of Bergen, Norway. 106: Museum of London. 107: Axel Poignant Archive, London. 108, 109: C. M. Dixon, Canterbury, Kent, England. 110, 111: *Tapisserie de Bayeux—XIe siècle. Avec autorisation spéciale de la ville de Bayeux.* 113-119: York Archeological Trust Historical Picture Library, York, England. 120: National Museum of Iceland, Reykjavík. 122: Mats Wibe Lund, Reykjavík, Iceland. 123: Map by Time-Life Books. 124, 125: Werner Forman Archive, London/ Stofnum Arna Magnussonar a Islandi, Reykjavík, Iceland. 126, 127: Department of Medieval Archaeology, Aarhus University, Denmark, photo Else Roesdahl, 1989; Standarholsbok AM 334, fol.37r/Stofnum Arna Magnussonar a Islandi, Reykjavík, Iceland. 128: Mats Wibe Lund, Reykjavík, Iceland. 129: © Mats Wibe Lund/National Museum of Iceland, Reykjavík. 130, 131: Dale M. Brown. 132: Birgitta Wallace, courtesy Canadian Parks Service. 134-141: Foto Kit Weiss, The National Museum, Copenhagen. 142, 143: Background Jonsbok, GKS 3269 fol.77v./Stofnum Arna Magnussonar a Islandi, Reykjavík, Iceland. Foto Kit Weiss, The National Museum, Copenhagen (4). 144: Greenland National Museum & Archives. 145: © Wolfgang Kaehler. 147: Courtesy Helge Ingstad, Oslo. 148: Stofnum Arna Magnussonar a Islandi, Reykjavík, Iceland; The Royal Library, Copenhagen—map by Time-Life Books. 149: Courtesy Helge Ingstad, Oslo. 150, 151: Courtesy Helge Ingstad, Oslo (2); D. Crawford, courtesy Canadian Parks Service (3)—S. Vandervlugt, courtesy Canadian Parks Service; Courtesy Helge Ingstad, Oslo. 152, 153: Birgitta Wallace, courtesy Canadian Parks Service—Birgitta Wallace, courtesy Canadian Parks Service—D. Crawford, courtesy Canadian Parks Service. 154, 155: André Cornellier, courtesy Canadian Parks Service; courtesy Canadian Parks Service. 156, 157: © Wolfgang Kaehler. 158, 159: Art by Paul Breeden.

BIBLIOGRAPHY

BOOKS:
Addyman, Peter. "The Attackers Return." In *The Vikings in England and in Their Danish Homeland*. London: Anglo-Danish Viking Project, 1981.
Almgren, Bertil. *The Viking*. Gothenburg, Sweden: Nordbok, 1975.

Andreasen, Claus, and Jette Arneborg. "The Farm beneath the Sand: New Investigations into Norsemen in Vesterbygd." In *Grønlandsk Kultur- og Samfunds Forskning 92*. Translated by Tim Davies. Nuuk, Greenland: Atuakkiorfik, 1992.
Arbman, Holger. *The Vikings*. Trans-

lated and edited by Alan Binns. New York: Frederick A. Praeger, 1961.
Arwidsson, Greta. *Valsgärde 7*. Uppsala: Uppsala Universitets Museum För Nordiska Fornsaker, 1977.
Atkinson, Ian. *The Viking Ships*. Cambridge: Cambridge University

Press, 1979.

Bibby, Geoffrey. "The Trail of the Vikings." In *Discovery of Lost Worlds*. Edited by Joseph J. Thorndike, Jr. New York: American Heritage, 1979.

Borg, Kaj, Ulf Näsman, and Erik Wegraeus. *The Monument* (Eketorp: Fortification and Settlement on Öland/Sweden series). Translated by Nils Stedt. Stockholm: Almquist & Wiksell International, 1976.

Bradley, John (Ed.). *The Viking Dublin Exposed: The Wood Quay Saga*. Dublin: O'Brien Press, 1984.

Brøgger, A. W., and Haakon Shetelig. *The Viking Ships: Their Ancestry and Evolution*. Oslo: Dreyers Forlag, 1971.

Brøgger, A. W., H. Falk, and H. Schetelig. "Burial of a Viking Queen." In *The Archaeologist at Work*. Harper & Row: New York, 1959.

Brøndsted, Johannes. *The Vikings*. Translated by Kalle Skov. Harmondsworth, England: Penguin Books, 1965.

Burks, John B. *Iceland in Pictures*. New York: Sterling Publishing, 1969.

Cant, Ronald G. "Settlement, Society and Church Organisation in the Northern Isles." In *The Northern and Western Isles in the Viking World*. Edited by Alexander Fenton and Hermann Pálsson. Edinburgh: John Donald Publishers, 1984.

Cohat, Yves. *The Vikings: Lords of the Seas*. London: Thames and Hudson, 1992.

Crawford, Barbara E. *Scandinavian Scotland*. Leicester: Leicester University Press, 1987.

Davidson, H. R. Ellis. *The Viking Road to Byzantium*. London: George Allen & Unwin, 1976.

Dixon, Philip. *The Making of the Past: Barbarian Europe*. New York: E. P. Dutton, 1976.

Edwards, Nancy. *The Archaeology of Early Medieval Ireland*. London: B. T. Batsford, 1990.

Eldjárn, Krístjan. "The Viking Myth." In *The Vikings*. Edited by R. T. Farrell. London: Phillimore, 1982.

Elliott, Ralph W. V. *Runes: An Introduction*. New York: St. Martin's Press, 1989.

Fellows-Jensen, Gillian. "Viking Settlement in the Northern and Western Isles—The Place-Name Evidence as Seen from Denmark and the Danelaw." In *The Northern and Western Isles in the Viking World*. Edited by Alexander Fenton and Hermann Pálsson. Edinburgh: John Donald Publishers, 1984.

Foote, Peter G., and David M. Wilson. *The Viking Achievement*. New York: Praeger, 1970.

Fury of the Northmen (TimeFrame series). Alexandria: Time-Life Books, 1988.

Gad, Finn. *The History of Greenland: Earliest Times to 1700*. London: C. Hurst, 1970.

Graham-Campbell, James. *The Viking World*. New Haven: Ticknor & Fields, 1980.

Graham-Campbell, James, and Dafydd Kidd. *The Vikings*. London: British Museum Publications, 1980.

Gregorietti, Guido. *Jewelry through the Ages*. New York: American Heritage, 1969.

Hall, Richard:
The Excavations at York: The Viking Dig. London: Bodley Head, 1984.
"A Late Pre-Conquest Urban Building Tradition." In *Archaeological Papers from York Presented to M. W. Barley*. Edited by P. V. Addyman and V. E. Black. York: York Archaeological Trust, 1984.
Viking Age Archaeology in Britain and Ireland. Buckinghamshire: Shire Publications, 1990.

Heath, Ian. *The Vikings*. London: Osprey, 1985.

Hødnebø, Finn, and Jónas Kristjánsson. *The Viking Discovery of America*. Translated by Elizabeth S. Seeberg. Oslo: J. M. Stenersens, 1991.

Ingstad, Anne Stine. *The Norse Discovery of America* (Vol. 1). Oslo: Norwegian University Press, 1985.

Ingstad, Helge:
Land under the Pole Star. New York: St. Martin's Press, 1966.
The Norse Discovery of America (Vol. 2). Oslo: Norwegian University Press, 1985.
Westward to Vinland. New York: St. Martin's Press, 1969.

Jansson, Sven B. F. *The Runes of Sweden*. Translated by Peter G. Foote.

Stockholm: P. A. Norstedt & Söners, 1962.

Jensen, Jörgen, Elisabeth Munksgaard, and Thorkild Ramskou. *Prehistoric Denmark*. Translated by David Liversage. Copenhagen: The National Museum, 1978.

Jesch, Judith. *Women in the Viking Age*. Suffolk: Boydell Press, 1991.

Jones, Gwyn:
A History of the Vikings. New York: Oxford University Press, 1984.
The Norse Atlantic Saga. New York: Oxford University Press, 1964.
"The Vikings and North America." In *The Vikings*. Edited by R. T. Farrell. London: Phillimore, 1982.

Kirkby, Michael Hasloch. *The Vikings*. Oxford: Phaidon, 1977.

Krogh, Knud J. *Viking Greenland*. Copenhagen: The National Museum, 1967.

La Fay, Howard. *The Vikings*. Washington, D.C.: National Geographic Society, 1972.

Logan, F. Donald. *The Vikings in History*. London: Hutchinson, 1983.

Lund, Niels. "Excerpts from the Anglo-Saxon Chronicle." In *The Vikings in England and in Their Danish Homeland*. London: Anglo-Danish Viking Project, 1981.

Magnusson, Magnus:
Viking: Hammer of the North. London: Orbis, 1976.
Vikings! London: BBC Books, 1980.

Magnusson, Magnus, and Hermann Pálsson (Transls.):
King Harald's Saga: Harald Hardradi of Norway. Harmondsworth, England: Penguin Books, 1966.
Njal's Saga. Harmondsworth, England: Penguin Books, 1960.
The Vinland Sagas. Harmondsworth, England: Penguin Books, 1965.

Morris, Christopher. "The Vikings in the British Isles: Some Aspects of Their Settlement and Economy." In *The Vikings*. Edited by R. T. Farrell. London: Phillimore, 1982.

Nørlund, Poul. *Viking Settlers in Greenland and Their Descendants during Five Hundred Years*. London: Cambridge University Press, 1936.

Olsen, Olaf, and Ole Crumlin-

Pedersen. *Five Viking Ships from Roskilde Fjord.* Translated by Barbara Bluestone. Copenhagen: The National Museum, 1985.

Oxenstierna, Eric:
The Norsemen. Translated and edited by Catherine Hutter. Greenwich, Conn.: New York Graphic Society, 1965.
The World of the Norsemen. Translated by Janet Sondheimer. Cleveland: World Publishing, 1967.

Page, R. I. *Runes.* Berkeley: University of California Press and the British Museum, 1987.

Pálsson, Hermann, and Paul Edwards. *Orkneyinga Saga: The History of the Earls of Orkney.* Harmondsworth, England: Penguin Books, 1981.

Payne, Blanche. *History of Costume: From the Ancient Egyptians to the Twentieth Century.* New York: Harper & Row, 1965.

Randsborg, Klavs. *The Viking Age in Denmark: The Formation of a State.* London: Duckworth, 1980.

Richards, Julian D. *English Heritage Book of Viking Age England.* London: B. T. Batsford, 1991.

Roberts, David. *Iceland: Land of the Sagas.* New York: Harry N. Abrams, 1990.

Roesdahl, Else. *The Vikings.* Translated by Susan M. Margeson and Kirsten Williams. Harmondsworth, England: Penguin Books, 1991.

Rying, Bent (Ed.). *Danish in the South and the North* (Vol. 1). Translated by Reginald Spink. Copenhagen: The Royal Danish Ministry of Foreign Affairs, 1981.

Sawyer, P. H.:
The Age of the Vikings. New York: St. Martin's Press, 1971.
Kings and Vikings: Scandinavia and Europe, AD 700-1100. New York: Methuen, 1982.

Sawyer, Peter. "The Causes of the Viking Age." In *The Vikings.* Edited by R. T. Farrell. London: Phillimore, 1982.

Shetelig, H., and H. Falk. "Royal Ship-Burials in Viking Times." In *The World of the Past.* Edited by Jacquetta Hawkes. New York: Alfred A. Knopf, 1963.

Simpson, Jacqueline. *Everyday Life in the Viking Age.* New York: G. P.

Putnam's, 1967.

Sjøvold, Thorleif. *The Viking Ships in Oslo.* Oslo: Universitetets Oldsaksamling, 1985.

Wahlgren, Erik. *The Vikings and America.* London: Thames and Hudson, 1986.

Wallace, Patrick. "The Archaeology of Viking Dublin." In *The Comparative History of Urban Origins in Non-Roman Europe: Ireland, Wales, Denmark, Germany, Poland and Russia from the Ninth to the Thirteenth Century.* Edited by H. B. Clarke and Anngret Simms. Oxford: B.A.R., 1985.

Wernick, Robert, and the Editors of Time-Life Books. *The Vikings* (The Seafarers series). Alexandria: Time-Life Books, 1979.

Wilson, David M. *The Vikings and Their Origins.* London: Thames and Hudson, 1970.

Wilson, David M., and Ole Klindt-Jensen. *Viking Art.* Minneapolis: University of Minnesota Press, 1980.

Wilson, David M. (Ed.). *The Northern World.* New York: Harry N. Abrams, 1980.

Yarwood, Doreen. *European Costume: 4000 Years of Fashion.* New York: Bonanza Books, 1982.

PERIODICALS:

Addyman, Peter V. "Eburacum, Jorvik, York." *Scientific American,* March 1980.

Arneborg, Jette. "The Roman Church in Norse Greenland." *Acta Archaeologica* (Copenhagen), Vol. 61, 1990.

Buckland, P. C. "A Paleoecological Study of the Impact of Landnám." *Acta Archaeologica* (Copenhagen), Vol. 61, 1990.

Christensen, Karen Marie Bojsen. "Aspects of the Norse Economy in the Western Settlement in Greenland." *Acta Archaeologica* (Copenhagen), Vol. 61, 1990.

Engelmark, Roger, and Karin Viklund. "Iron Age Agriculture (Land Use) in Norrland." *Populär Arkeologi,* June 15-20, 1986.

Hall, Richard. "The Vikings as Town-Dwellers." *History Today,* November 1986.

Ingstad, Helge. "Vinland Ruins Prove

Vikings Found the New World." *National Geographic,* November 1964.

Jones, Gwyn. "The Viking World: An Address to the Conference." *Acta Archaeologica* (Copenhagen), Vol. 61, 1990.

Jordan, Robert Paul. "Viking Trail East." *National Geographic,* March 1985.

Keller, Christian. "Vikings in the West Atlantic: A Model of Norse Greenlandic Medieval Society." *Acta Archaeologica* (Copenhagen), Vol. 61, 1990.

McGovern, Thomas H.:
"Climate, Correlation, and Causation in Norse Greenland." *Arctic Anthropology,* Vol. 28, no. 2, 1991.
"Cows, Harp Seals, and Churchbells: Adaptation and Extinction in Norse Greenland." *Human Ecology,* Vol. 8, no. 3, 1980.
"The Vinland Adventure: A North Atlantic Perspective." *North American Archaeologist,* Vol. 2, no. 4, 1980-81.

Ogilvie, Astrid E. J. "Climatic Changes in Iceland A.D. c. 865 to 1598." *Acta Archaeologica* (Copenhagen), Vol. 61, 1990.

Wallace, Birgitta Linderoth:
"The Kensington Stone." *The Old Northwest,* Winter 1984-1985.
"L'Anse aux Meadows: Gateway to Vinland." *Acta Archaeologica* (Copenhagen), Vol. 61, 1990.

Wilford, John Noble. "Norsemen in America Flourished Then Faded." *New York Times,* July 7, 1992.

OTHER:

Amorosi, Thomas. "Climate Impact and Human Response in Northeast Iceland: Archaeological Investigations at Svalbard, 1986-1988." Report. New York: Hunter College of the City University of New York, October 1991.

"From Viking to Crusader: The Scandinavians and Europe, 800-1200." Catalog. New York: Rizzoli, 1992.

Ingstad, Anne Stine. "The Norse Settlement of L'Anse aux Meadows, Newfoundland." Symposium papers. Edited by Eleanor Guralnick. Chicago: The Archaeological Institute of America and the Museum of

Science and Industry of Chicago, April 3, 1982.

Ingstad, Helge. "The Discovery of a Norse Settlement in America." Symposium papers. Edited by Eleanor Guralnick. Chicago: The Archaeological Institute of America and the Museum of Science and Industry of Chicago, April 3, 1982.

Jones, Gwyn. "Historical Evidence for Viking Voyages to the New World." Symposium papers. Edited by Eleanor Guralnick. Chicago: The Archaeological Institute of America and the Museum of Science and Industry of Chicago, April 3, 1982.

McGovern, Thomas H. "The Lost Norse Colony of Greenland." Symposium papers. Edited by Eleanor Guralnick. Chicago: The Archaeological Institute of America and the Museum of Science and Industry of Chicago, April 3, 1982.

The Vikings in England and in Their Danish Homeland. Catalog. London: The Anglo-Danish Viking Project, 1981.

INDEX

Christ Church Cathedral (Dublin):
preservationist rally at, *96*
Christensen, Karen Marie: 134
Clontarf, battle of: 112
Cnut: unification of English kingdoms by, 110-111, 159
Codex Aureus: *92, 93*
Coins: Arabic, *50,* 52, 64, 65; Byzantine, 64; English, 101, 108; Frankish, 58; Frisian, 54; and hoards, 52, 55; Irish, 101; iron die for, *117;* Islamic, *67;* mints, 101, 117; Norse, *117,* 133, *159;* Roman, 12, *13*
Coll: 106
Colonsay: 104
Colton: 107
Common futhark: *28*
Connaught: 97
Constantine VII Porphyrogenitus: 70, 71
Constantinople: 64, 76; trade route to, 68, 70-72; Viking assaults on, 72-73, 159
Copenhagen: 142
Coppergate: excavations at, *113-119*
Córdoba: 27
Cork: 100
Corpse Lodinn: 137
Craftwork: molds used for, *55*
Cuerdale hoard: *100-101,* 108

D

Dalby: 90
Danegelds: 58, 108-109
Danelaw: 90, 95, 107-108
Danish futhark: *28*
Danish National Museum: 39, 46
Danube River: 72, 74
Davis Strait: 147
Decker, George: 148, *150*
Denmark: eastern trade by, 159
Derby: 107
Dir: 70
Disko Bay: 136, 138
Dnepropetrovsk: 71
Dnieper River: 64, 67, 68, 69, 70, 71, 74, 76, 159
Dniester River: 72
Don River: 65
Dorestad: Viking raids on, 54, 158
Dublin: 101; excavations in, 97-100; preservation protests at Wood Quay site, *96;* trade center, 56, 100, 101, 108; Viking base at, 93, 112
du Chatellier, Paul: 57
Dumbarton Rock: 103

E

East Anglia: 94, 110
Eastern Settlement: 132, 136, 137, 144-146, 159
Ed: rune-stone found at, 75
Edward the Confessor: 76
Egede, Neils: 145
Einar Sokkeson: 137
Eindridi Jonsson: 136
Eirik's Saga: 147, 148, 149
Eiriks Fjord: *130,* 132
Eirik the Red: 123, 134, 146, 147; banishment from Iceland, 129; death of, 133; discovery and settlement of Greenland, 131-132, 159; Greenland farm site of, *131,* 137, 138
Eirik Thorvaldsson Raudi: *See* Eirik the Red
Eketorp: excavations at, *59*
England: and Danelaw, 90, 95, 107-108; Norman conquest of, 17, 90, 112; Roman road network in, 94; Viking raids on, 87-88, 94-95, 109-110, 159; Viking settlements in, 90, *map* 91, 95, 107-108, 113
Eoforwic: 113, 114
Epaves Bay: 150
Erling Sighvatsson: 136
Ermentarius: 60
Eskimos: *See* Inuits
Exeter: 94, 101
Eymund the Fisherman: *98-99*

F

Faeroe Islands: 121, *map* 123
Fiesole: 55
Flateyjarbok: 125
Floki, Raven: 123, 124, 125, 159
Foss River: 94, 118
France: 52; trade with, 16; Viking lodgements in, 17, 57-58, 158
Frankish empire: 52
Franks: 27
Frey (deity): 30, 56
Frisia: 52; Viking raids in, 54, 60, 158
Fryton: 90
Futharks: 28
Fyn: 81
Fyrkat: Viking fort at, 58, *59*

G

Gaia: 32-33
Gairsay: 103
Gardar: bishopric at, 137; excavations at, *138-139*
Gardar Svavarsson: 123

Gaut Biornsson: 106
Gijon: 55
Gjermundbu: 34
Gnezdovo: 70; Viking burial mounds at, *68-69*
Gnezdovo silver hoard: *68*
Godafoss: *128*
Godar: 125
Godfred (king): 58
Gokstad: excavation of burial ship, 9-10, *11,* 14, 23
Gorodishche: artifacts found at, *65*
Gotland: 12, 54, 65, 79; picture stone found at, *31, 158;* trade center, 27, 64
Gragas (legal code): 126, *127*
Grani: 72
Grave goods: 12, *17,* 18, *19-21, 22, 23, 26, 27,* 38, 51-52, 53, *65, 70-71,* 90, 97-98, 104, *105*
Graverobbers: 10, 18
Great Dragon: 76
Greenland: 32, 112, *map* 123, 147; disappearance of Viking colony in, 140-142, 145-146; environmental difficulties at, 138, 140-141; estimated population of, 132, 144; excavation of cemetery in, *134, 135;* naming of, 131-132; trade with, 136; Viking colonies in, 17, 44, 121-122, 131-139, 140-146, 158
Greenlanders' Saga: 133, 147, *148,* 150
Greenland Museum: 140
Grimston: 107
Grobin: 65
Guadalquivir River: 55
Gudrod of Vestvold: 14
Gulf of Finland: fur trade in, 53
Gulf of St. Lawrence: Viking exploration of, 152
Gunnbjörn: 129
Gustafson, Gabriel: excavation of Oseberg ship, *16,* 18-23
Guthfrith: 106
Guthrum: 95, 106

H

Hack silver: 101
Hagia Sophia: runic inscriptions in, *73, 75*
Halfdan: 103
Hanseatic League: 139
Harald (brother of Cnut): 110
Harald Bluetooth: 36, 58, 82, 83
Harald Fairhair: 22, 122
Harald Hardraade: 35-36, 112; and Varangian Guard, 75-76
Harald Sigurdsson: 75-76. *See also*

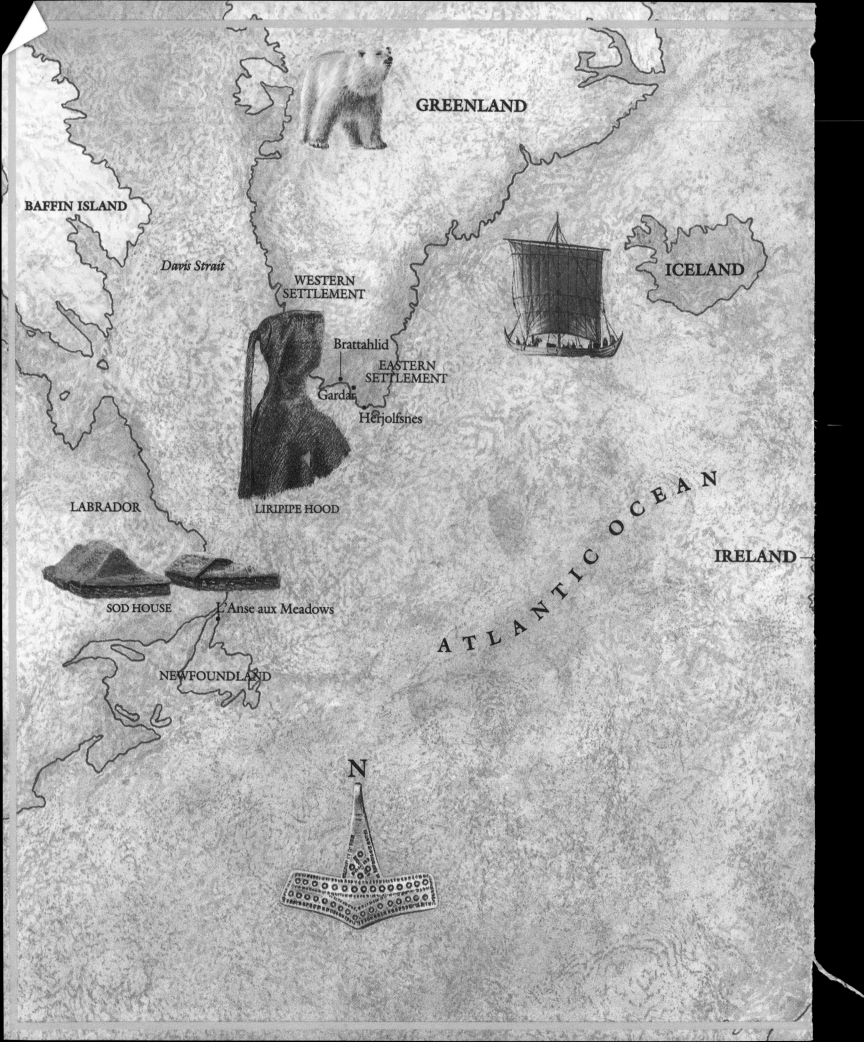

GREENLAND

BAFFIN ISLAND

Davis Strait

ICELAND

WESTERN
SETTLEMENT

Brattahlid

EASTERN
SETTLEMENT

Gardar

Herjolfsnes

LIRIPIPE HOOD

LABRADOR

ATLANTIC OCEAN

IRELAND

SOD HOUSE   L'Anse aux Meadows

NEWFOUNDLAND

N